BLACK & DECKER

THE COMPLETE GUIDE TO
LANDSCAPE CONSTRUCTION

60 Step-by-Step Projects for Creating a Perfect Landscape

Creative Publishing international

CHANHASSEN, MINNESOTA
www.creativepub.com

Contents

Creative Publishing
international

Copyright © 2006
Creative Publishing international, Inc.
18705 Lake Drive East
Chanhassen, Minnesota 55317
1-800-328-3895
www.creativepub.com
All rights reserved

Printed in China

10 9 8 7 6 5 4 3 2 1

President/CEO: Ken Fund

Publisher: Bryan Trandem
Assistant Managing Editor: Tracy Stanley
Senior Editor: Mark Johanson
Senior Art Directors: Dave Schelitzche, Jon Simpson
Photo Editor: Julie Caruso
Creative Director, Photography: Tim Himsel
Lead Photographer: Steve Galvin
Scene Shop Carpenter: Randy Austin
Editors: Tom Lemmer, Andrew Karrre
Contributing Writers: Paul Gorton, Sid Korpi
Proofreader: Chuck Pederson
Additional Photography: Andrea Rugg
Production Manager: Laura Hokkanen

THE COMPLETE GUIDE TO LANDSCAPE CONSTRUCTION
Created by: The Editors of Creative Publishing international, Inc., in
cooperation with Black & Decker. Black & Decker® is a trademark of
The Black & Decker Corporation and is used under license.

Library of Congress Cataloging-in-Publication Data

The complete guide to landscape construction : 60 step-by-step projects for creating a perfect landscape / Black & Decker.
   p. cm.
  Summary: "Includes projects ranging from basic earthmoving and yard shaping to creating privacy fences, pathways and watercourses. Features the latest in tools, techniques, products and materials, including vinyl fencing, tumbled retaining wall block and outdoor fireplaces"--Provided by publisher.
  Includes index.
  ISBN-13: 978-1-58923-245-7 (soft cover)
  ISBN-10: 1-58923-245-3 (soft cover)
  1. Landscape construction. I. Black & Decker Corporation (Towson, Md.)
  TH4961.C654 2006
  712'.6--dc22

2005036021

Introduction

Your yard offers enormous opportunities to improve the value of your home and the quality of your life. Real estate experts say that an improved landscape can add as much as 20 percent to the property value of a home. And a remodeled landscape can create new living space for you and your family, effectively making your house larger than before.

With *The Complete Guide to Landscape Construction*, you'll learn how to create 50 popular features for yourself. And although building landscape features can be hard work, there are two very important reasons to do your own landscape construction.

First, you can save lots of money. Because most of the expense in a landscape renovation is the physical labor, you can save hundreds, if not thousands, of dollars by doing this work yourself—often on one project alone.

But believe it or not, the second reason for tackling DIY landscaping might be even more important: personal satisfaction. Landscape projects offer visible, tangible results more dramatic than almost any other home improvement project. A month after creating an elegant raised bed from natural stone, you'll have neighbors stopping in to admire your work. Guests will admire the meandering stone pathway and rose arbor you've created. After a long day at work, you'll have a sheltered arbor where you can kick back and relax.

Landcape construction can even be fun. Why go to the gym and spend hours on a treadmill, when you can enjoy fresh air, work up a healthy sweat, create something beautiful and amazing, and save money—all at the same time?

The book you're holding is a comprehensive do-it-yourself manual for creating all the features that make a functional and beautiful landscape. The projects found here include both the hidden (underground sprinkler systems) and the highly visible (arbors and ornamental fences), and everything in between.

There are hundreds of books and magazines that help people dream about gorgeous landscapes, but they often speak to the world of dreams, not the world of reality. Finding ideas for your landscape is amazingly easy; learning how to make these ideas real is much more challenging. Until now.

This book will be useful whether you are creating a landscape from scratch, looking to renovate an old landscape, or simply wanting to make spot improvements here and there. Newly constructed homes often have no real landscaping at all. This book is an ideal guide if you're looking to turn a flat, stark suburban lawn into a rolling landscape with real outdoor living space. On the other hand, if you have a smaller, innercity landscape, creating a rock garden, raised planting beds, a small patio, masonry garden walls, and a drip irrigation system can create delightful escape from the frenzy of city life.

The information in this book comes from firsthand experience. All the writers, editors, and workers contributing to this book have done these projects for themselves, aided by landscape professionals who often worked side by side with them. Many of the projects in this book were written, literally, with fresh dirt under the fingernails. It's the voice of experience you'll hear on the following pages.

And now, let's get started creating your dream landscape.

NOTICE TO READERS

For safety, use caution, care, and good judgment when following the procedures described in this book. The publisher and Black & Decker cannot assume responsibility for any damage to property or injury to persons as a result of misuse of the information provided.

The techniques shown in this book are general techniques for various applications. In some instances, additional techniques not shown in this book may be required. Always follow manufacturers' safety warnings and instructions included with products. Deviation from the directions may create injury exposure and void warranties. The projects in this book vary widely as to skill levels required. Some may not be appropriate for all do-it-yourselfers, and some may require professional help.

Consult your local building department for information on building permits, codes, and other laws as they apply to your project.

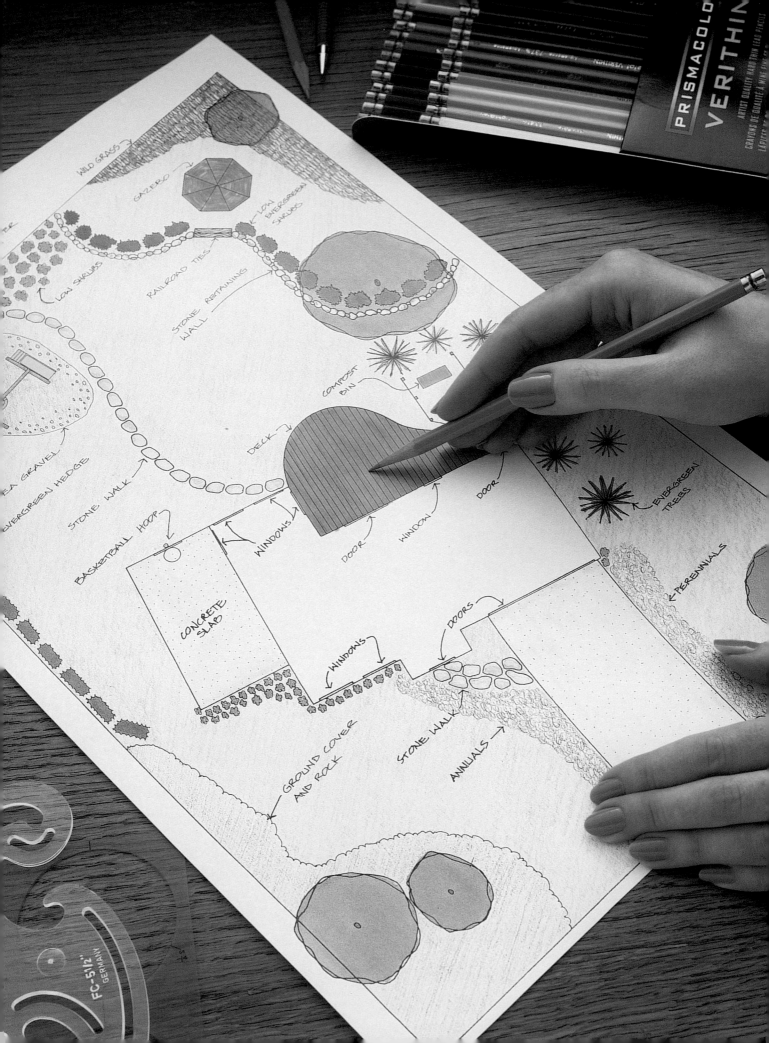

Before You Begin

In this section, you'll find background reference materials that you may find helpful when planning individual projects or when creating a master plan for your overall landscape. It contains information on the building materials used in landscaping, how to estimate those materials, and the tools and hardware used. It also includes a summary of the important building code requirements and other issues to keep in mind when planning the elements of your landscape.

Landscapes tend to evolve over time. It's not uncommon for a do-it-yourselfer to take several years to complete all the landscape work, so it's also important to give some thought to the "big picture" when planning each project. It's a very good idea to spend some time right now thinking about the ultimate goal of your landscape, considering how each piece will fit into the whole. With this in mind, the last project in this section will show you how to sketch out a master plan for your landscape. This plan will become the blueprint for your finished landscape, the road map you use to plan and organize all your landscaping projects.

• **Building materials** (page 8).

• **Estimating & ordering materials** (page 16).

• **Tools** (page 18).

• **Codes & considerations** (page 22).

• **Drawing plans** (page 26).

Cedar

Pressure-treated pine

Redwood

Pine

Cedar lattice

Bark mulch

Building Materials

Many landscape projects can be built from a variety of building materials. A retaining wall, for example, can be created from wood timbers, from concrete block, or from natural stone. A patio can be made from poured concrete, from flagstone, or from brick. Your choice of materials will be based on style and appearance, but also on cost, durability, and ease of installation. Carefully consider all these issues when choosing the materials you'll use.

Lumber

Wood is the single most popular building material for outdoor construction, for obvious reasons: it's versatile, easy to work with, and relatively inexpensive when compared to stone, brick, or composite materials. These properties make it ideal for many structures, such as fences, arbors, and decks. Bark, wood chips, and shredded wood are used for loose-fill material around shrubs and in planting areas and in pathways. Most home centers and lumberyards carry a wide selection of dimension lumber from which you can build anything you want, but to make your work easier, look for the wide variety of pre-assembled and precut products now available, such as fence panels, premilled posts, pickets, railings, and stairway parts.

The problem with wood in outdoor construction is that it eventually will decay—sooner rather than later in wet climates. Of the common species available in most lumberyards, only cedar, redwoods and woods that are pressure-treated with pesticides are suitable. Untreated pine, spruce, and fir—the varieties used for most indoor construction—are suitable for outdoor use only in the most arid of climates.

Redwood and cedar are attractive, relatively soft woods with a natural resistance to moisture and insects—ideal qualities for outdoor applications. Pressure-treated pine is stronger and more durable than redwood or cedar and is more readily available and less expensive in many areas. For framing members that are in contact with the ground, though, you should always use pressure-treated lumber.

No matter what type or grade of lumber you select, inspect each board for flaws before buying it. Reject any that are warped or that have cracks or large knots.

Framing lumber—typically pine or pressure-treated pine—comes in a few different grades: "select structural" (SEL STR), "construction" (CONST) or "standard" (STAND), and "utility" (UTIL). For most applications, construction grade no. 2 offers the best balance between quality and price. Utility grade is a lower-cost lumber suitable for nonstructural members. Board lumber, or finish lumber, is graded by quality and appearance, with the main criterion being the number and size of knots present. "Clear" pine, for example, has no knots

Up until a few years ago, arsenic and chromium were the chemicals used in pressure-treated pine. These chemicals had well-documented health risks, and lumber treated this way needed to be handled carefully. Fortunately, the pressure-treated lumber now sold gets its insect- and rot-resistance from different chemicals—ammoniacal copper quarternary (ACQ) is the most common. While it's always a good idea to handle pressure-treated lumber carefully, these new products are much safer.

The new chemicals, however, can corrode standard nails and screws very quickly, so make sure you use the fasteners recommended by the wood manufacturer. Stainless steel fasteners are the preferred choice.

Although cedar and pressure-treated pine resist rotting, they won't survive indefinitely Periodically treat your projects with a wood sealer/preservative. Choose a product from a well-known manufacturer and apply the product every 2 years.

Apply a coat of sealer to all sides of outdoor projects For smaller projects brush the product on. For larger decks and structures, use a pressure sprayer.

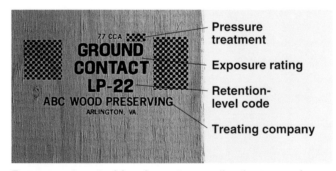

Pressure-treated lumber stamps list the type of preservative and the chemical retention level, as well as the exposure rating and the name and location of the treating company.

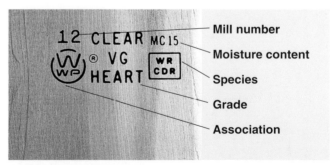

Cedar grade stamps list the mill number, moisture content, species, lumber grade, and membership association. Western red cedar (WRC) or incense cedar (INC) for decks should be heartwood (HEART) with a maximum moisture content of 15% (MC15).

Metals

Metal of various types is often used for fences and gates. Aluminum offers a sturdy, lightweight, and waterproof material that is available in a variety of designs. Aluminum is also a popular material for lamp posts. Galvanized chain-link steel is also a popular choice for fencing, because it is relatively maintenance free and reasonably priced. Chain link is also a good choice where security is a concern. Traditional wrought iron, though more expensive, is used for fencing, railings, gates, and patio furniture.

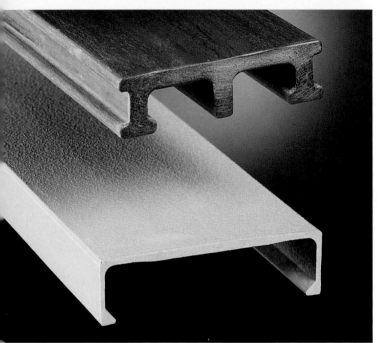

Plastics

Plastic materials such as PVC vinyl and fiberglass reinforced plastic (FRP) are generally used in applications such as fencing, arbors, deck skirting, and lawn edging. Many styles and sizes are available, and they are strong, versatile, and require no maintenance. Some fence materials are sold as kits, making installation easy.

Landscape fabric controls weed growth in and around your project area.

Composite Materials

Composite materials blend together wood fibers and plastics to create a rigid product that will not rot, splinter, warp, or crack. These boards can be cut with a circular saw, require little to no maintenance, and don't need to be painted or stained. Although they're typically more expensive than wood and other alternatives, composites are extremely durable and over the life of a structure can be less expensive than wood, which may need to be replaced. Composites are a good choice for decking, railing systems, and landscaping timbers.

Manufactured Stone

Manufactured stone is designed to resemble natural stone, but because it's more uniform it is easier to install and generally costs less. Brick, concrete, and glass block are being offered in more styles all the time, giving you a lot of flexibility to build distinctive projects that are also reasonably priced. Decorative concrete block can be used to make screen walls and is available in many colors.

Concrete paver slabs, available in several shapes and sizes, are used for laying simple walkways and patios. They're available in a standard finish, a smooth aggregate finish, or can be colored and molded to resemble brick. Concrete paver slabs are relatively inexpensive and quite easy to work with. They're usually laid in a bed of sand and require no mortar. Their surface is generally finished so the smooth gravel aggregate is exposed, but they are also available in plain pavers and aggregate.

Paver bricks resemble traditional kiln-dried clay bricks but are more durable and easier to install. Paver bricks come in many colors and shapes and are ideal for paving patios, walkways, and driveways. Many varieties are available in interlocking shapes that can be combined with standard bricks to create decorative patterns, such as herringbone and basket weave. Edging blocks are precast in different sizes for creating boundaries to planting areas, lawns, loose-fill paths, and retaining walls.

Interlocking retaining wall blocks

Molded paver slabs

Paver bricks

Exposed aggregate paver slabs

Concrete paver slabs

Brick and concrete block are available in a growing variety of sizes and styles, allowing you to build distinctive outdoor structures.

Fieldstone is stone gathered from fields, dry riverbeds, and hillsides. It is used in wall construction.

Flagstone consists of large slabs of quarried stone cut into pieces up to 3" thick. It is used in walks, steps, and patios.

A stone yard is a great place to get ideas and see the types of stone that are available. This stone yard includes a display area that identifies different types of stone and suggests ways they can be used.

Natural stone offers beautiful color, interesting texture, and great durability, making it one of the very best building materials for outdoor construction. Although it is more expensive than many other materials, if it fits in your budget, you're not likely to regret choosing stone. It is a good choice for edging, walls, walkways, ponds, fountains, and waterfalls. Natural stone is also used to accent flowers and plants creating depth in garden areas (this is a great way to use stone if you can't afford huge amounts of it).

Each type of stone offers a distinctive look, as well as a specific durability and workability. The nature of your project will often dictate the best form of stone to use. When shopping for stone, describe your project to the supplier and ask him or her to suggest a stone that meets your needs.

Fieldstone sometimes called river rock, is used to build retaining walls, ornamental garden walls, and rock gardens. When split into smaller pieces, fieldstone can be used in projects with mortar. When cut into small pieces, or quarried stone, fieldstone is called cobblestone, a common material in walks and paths.

Ashlar or wall stone, is quarried granite, marble, or limestone that has been smooth-cut into large blocks, ideal for creating clean lines with thin mortar joints. Cut stone works well for stone garden walls, but because of its expense, its use is sometimes limited to decorative wall caps.

Flagstone is large slabs of sedimentary rock with naturally flat surfaces. Limestone, sandstone, slate, and shale are the most common types of flagstone. It is usually cut into pieces up to 3" thick, for use in walks, steps, and patios. Smaller pieces—less than 16" square—are often called steppers.

Veneer stone is natural or manufactured stone cut or molded for use in nonload-bearing, cosmetic applications, such as facing exterior walls or freestanding concrete block walls.

Rubble is irregular pieces of quarried stone, usually with one split or finished face. It is widely used in wall construction.

Concrete

Poured concrete is used for driveways, walk-ways, and patios because of its exceptional strength. Although it is sometimes criticized for its bland appearance, concrete in modern use is often tinted or given a surface finish that lets it simulate brick pavers or flagstone at a fraction of the cost. Concrete can also be formed into curves and other shapes, such as landscape ponds or fountains.

Concrete is made up of a mixture of portland cement, sand, coarse gravel, and water, and you can, if you choose, buy these raw ingredients and mix concrete yourself. For smaller projects, though, you'll find it more practical to buy pre-mixed bags of dry concrete

For small projects, prepare bagged concrete mix in a wheelbarrow or plastic trough. For mixing larger amounts from raw ingredients, rent a power mixer.

Another option for large projects, such as a driveway or patio slab, is to have premixed concrete delivered by a ready-mix supplier. If you choose this method, make sure you have plenty of help on hand to move and finish the concrete quickly.

Mortar

Mortar is a mixture of portland cement, fine sand, and water, used to "glue" stone and concrete materials together. Other ingredients, such as lime and gypsum, are added to improve workability or control setup time.

Every mortar mixture is designed for a specific purpose; make sure you choose the right one.

Type N is a medium-strength mortar for above-grade outdoor use in nonload-bearing (free-standing) walls, barbecues, chimneys, soft stone masonry, and tuck-pointing.

Type S is a high-strength mortar used for outdoor use at or below ground level. It is generally used in foundations, brick-and-block retaining walls, driveways, walks, and patios.

Type M is a very high-strength specialty mortar for load-bearing exterior stone walls, including stone retaining walls and veneer applications.

Glass block mortar is a specialty white type S mortar for glass block projects. Standard gray type S mortar is also acceptable.

Premixed concrete products contain all the components of concrete. Just add water, mix, and pour.

To mix concrete ingredients in a wheelbarrow, use a ratio of 1 part portland cement (A), 2 parts sand (B), and 3 parts coarse gravel (C).

Prepackaged mortar mixes are available at home centers. Simply select the proper mortar mixture for your project, mix in water, and start to trowel.

Refractory mortar is a calcium aluminate mortar that does not break down with exposure to high temperatures; it is used for mortaring around firebrick in fireplaces and barbecues.

Chemical-set mortar will cure even in wet conditions.

Hardware & Fasteners

Although they're rarely visible, the metal brackets, screws, nails, bolts, and other hardware items can be crucial to a successful landscaping project.

Metal anchors are a common type of hardware used for landscape projects and decks. Some of the most common types are shown in the photo below. Used to reinforce framing connections, many of the anchors called for in the various projects (and all of the anchors in the sheds and outbuilding projects) are Simpson Strong-Tie brand, which are commonly available at lumberyards and home centers. If you can't find what

you need on the shelves, look through the manufacturer's catalog, or visit their Web site (see page 235). Always use the fasteners recommended by the manufacturer.

The chemicals now used in pressure-treated lumber may require metal connectors specially designed to withstand the corrosive effect of these chemicals. Specifically, manufacturers suggest that metal connectors used with pressure-treated lumber be galvanized with a hot-dip process rather than a mechanical zinc plating. Triple-dipped, hot-dipped galvanized fasters are the best.

Alternatively, you can use stainless steel fasteners with pressure-treated lumber. Do not use aluminum fasteners with pressure-treated lumber.

Nails, screws, bolts, washers, nuts, and lag screws for outdoor use must be resistant to corrosion. Generally, metals are coated with some additional material to make them weatherproof. You may see products coated with materials like epoxy and ceramic. But the best choice may be the old standby—galvanized steel.

Galvanized steel has a zinc coating. If you are working with pressure-treated lumber, it's important that the nails, screws, bolts, and other fasteners be

Metal connectors commonly used include: Joist hanger (A), flashing (B), angled joist hanger (C), adjustable post beam cap (D), nonadjustable post cap (E), seismic tie (F), H-fit tie (G), post anchor with washer and pedestal (H), stair cleat (I), joist tie (J), angle bracket (K).

double or triple hot-dipped, a process that improves and thickens the bond between the zinc and steel. Look for the phrase *hot-dipped* or HDG on the package when buying galvanized hardware.

Stainless steel is the other common alternative when working with pressure-treated lumber. Although these fasteners are somewhat expensive, they have excellent weather resistance.

When working with composite lumber, use the fasteners recommended by the lumber manufac-turer. "Composite" screws often are designed with a special head shape that prevents the screws from mushrooming when driven into composite material.

There are a number of head-driving options available for exterior-rated screws. Square and torx-drive screws will not slip while fastening like phillips heads. Posit-drive screws are very popular because they combine phillips and square-drive heads, giving you a choice of which to use.

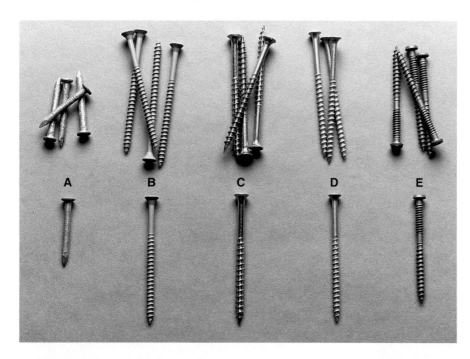

Specialty nails and screws for landscaping projects include: Metal connector nails (A), color-plated screws (B), Stainless steel screws (C), galvanized screws (D), composite screws (E). Composite screws have a slightly different head and thread configuration.

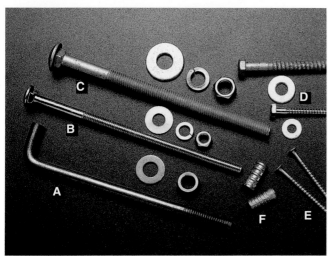

Common fasteners include: J-bolt with nut and washer (A), carriage bolts with washers and nuts (B, C), galvanized lag screws and washers (D), corrosion-resistant deck screws (E), masonry anchors (F).

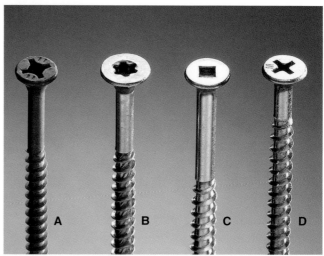

Head styles for exterior screws include: Posit-drive (A), torx (B), square drive (C), and phillips (D).

Estimating & Ordering Materials

Even with small projects, it's important to take careful measurements and estimate accurately. Landscaping materials are bulky and are expensive and time consuming to transport, so accurate estimating will save you time and money.

Begin compiling a materials list by reviewing the scale drawing of your building plans (pages 26 to 29). then use the information here to estimate materials. Once you have developed a materials list, add 10 percent to the estimate for each item to allow for waste and small oversights.

You might want to buy a contractor's calculator to help convert measurements and estimate concrete volume. The calculator isn't very expensive and will relieve you of complex math conversions. It's also handy for estimating fencing materials and paint coverage.

The cost of your project will depend upon which building materials you choose. You can save money by choosing materials that are readily available in your area. This is particularly true of natural stone products. Choosing stone that is quarried locally is far less expensive than exotic stone transported long distances. Lumber, metal, and plastics can also vary widely in price, depending on where it's milled or manufactured.

Most of what you need is available at large, general-purpose home centers, but for landscaping projects you may want to buy some materials from specialty retailers. A large concrete project, for example, will be cheaper if you buy ready-mix concrete instead of bagged concrete mix from your home center.

If you plan on working with specialty or alternative materials, such as vinyl fencing or composite decking, many home centers will have a select range of styles and sizes on hand but can also order specialty materials for you.

How to Estimate Materials

Sand, gravel, topsoil (2" layer)	surface area (sq. ft.) ÷ 100 = tons needed
Standard brick pavers for walks (2" layer)	surface area (sq. ft.) × 5 = number of pavers needed
Standard bricks for walls and pillars (4 × 8")	surface area (sq. ft.) × 7 = number of bricks needed (single brick thickness)
Poured concrete (4" layer)	surface area (sq. ft.) × .012 = cubic yards needed
Flagstone	surface area (sq. ft.) ÷ 100 = tons needed
Interlocking block (2" layer)	area of wall face (sq. ft.) × 1.5 = number of stones needed
Ashlar stone for 1-ft.-thick walls	area of wall face (sq. ft.) ÷ 15 = tons of stone needed
Rubble stone for 1-ft.-thick walls	area of wall face (sq. ft.) ÷ 35 = tons of stone needed
8 × 8 × 16" concrete block for freestanding walls	height of wall (ft.) × length of wall (ft.) × 1.125 = number of blocks needed

Ingrown knot

Inspect lumber for flaws. Sight along each board to check for warping and twisting. Return any boards with serious flaws. Check for loose knots. Boards used for structural parts should have only small knots that are tight and ingrown.

Amount of concrete needed (cubic feet)

Number of 8"- diameter footings	Depth of footings (feet)			
	1	2	3	4
2	¾	1½	2¼	3
3	1	2¼	3½	4½
4	1½	3	4½	6
5	2	3¾	5¾	7½

DRY INGREDIENTS FOR SELF-MIX

Amount of concrete needed (cubic feet)	94-lb. bags of portland cement	Cubic feet of sand	Cubic feet of gravel	60-lb. bags of premixed dry concrete
1	⅙	⅓	½	2
2	⅓	⅔	1	4
3	½	1½	3	6
4	¾	1¾	3½	8
5	1	2¼	4½	10
10	2	4½	9	20

Local brick and stone suppliers will often help you design your project and advise you about estimating materials, local building codes, and climate considerations.

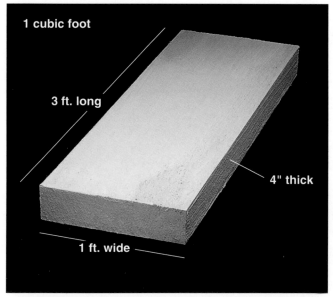

1 cubic foot
3 ft. long
4" thick
1 ft. wide

To estimate concrete volume, measure the width and length of the project in feet, then multiply the dimensions to get the square footage. Measure the thickness in feet (4" thick equals ⅓ ft.), then multiply the square footage times the thickness to get the cubic footage. For example, 1 ft. × 3 ft. × ⅓ ft. = 1 cu. ft. Twenty-seven cubic feet equals 1 cubic yard.

CONCRETE COVERAGE

Volume	Thickness	Surface coverage
1 cu. yd.	2"	160 sq. ft.
1 cu. yd.	3"	110 sq. ft.
1 cu. yd.	4"	80 sq. ft.
1 cu. yd.	5"	65 sq. ft.
1 cu. yd.	6"	55 sq. ft.
1 cu. yd.	8"	40 sq. ft.

Hand tools include: caulk gun (A), tape measure (B), chalk line (C), compass (D), garden hose (E), bow saw (F), plumb bob (G), combination square (H), speed square (I), pressure sprayer (J), mason's line (K), square and round shovels (M), garden rake (N), posthole digger (O), hoe (P), carpenter's level (Q), framing square (R), putty knife (S), wood chisel (T), awl (U), socket wrench (V), hammer (W), rubber mallet (X), pruning shears (Y), metal shears (Z), bar clamps (AA), and pipe clamps (BB).

Tools

Landscaping projects can require quite a few tools, sometimes including large specialty tools. The photos here show the tools used for the projects in this book.

You probably already own many of the common tools, but for the specialty tools it may be best to borrow or rent them as the need arises. Rental centers carry a full line of power tools and equipment that can take the time and extensive labor out of a larger project.

Basic Hand Tools

Basic hand tools for outdoor building projects should be rated for heavy-duty construction. If you buy new tools, invest in good ones, which will perform better and last longer. Metal tools should be made from high-carbon steel with

smoothly finished surfaces. Hand tools should be well balanced and have tight, comfortably molded handles.

Masonry Tools

Most masonry work requires specialty tools, many of which you'll need to buy or rent. To lay concrete you will need trowels, floats, edgers, and jointers. These are hand tools used to place, shape, and finish concrete and mortar. Chisels are used to cut and fit brick and block, You can also equip your circular saw with blades and your power drill with bits designed for use with concrete and brick.

Always make sure you have the necessary safety equipment on hand before you start a masonry project, including gloves and protective eyewear.

Mason's tools you may need for concrete work include: a darby (A) for smoothing screeded concrete; mortar hawk (B) for holding mortar; pointing trowel (C) for tuck-pointing stone mortar; wide pointing tool (D) for tuck-pointing or placing mortar on brick and block walls; jointer (E) for finishing mortar joints; brick tongs (F) for carrying multiple bricks; narrow tuck-pointer (G) for tuck-pointing or placing mortar on brick and block walls; mason's trowel (H) for applying mortar; masonry chisels (I) for splitting brick, block, and stone; bullfloat (J) for floating large slabs; mason's hammers (K) for chipping brick and stone; maul (L) for driving stakes; square-end trowel (M) for concrete finishing; side edger (N) and step edger (O) for finishing inside and outside corners of concrete; joint chisel (P) for removing dry mortar; control jointer (Q) for creating control joints; tile nippers (R) for trimming tile; sled jointer (S) for smoothing long joints; steel trowel (T) for finishing concrete; magnesium or wood float (U) for floating concrete; screed board (V) for screeding concrete.

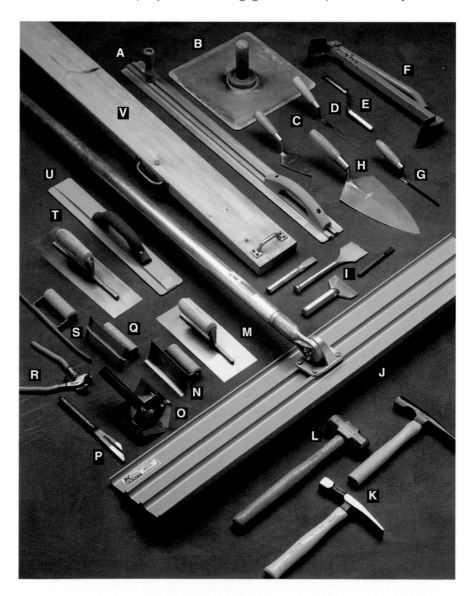

Power tools include: power miter saw (A), circular saw (B), drill with bits (C), reciprocating saw (D), jig saw (E), hammer drill and bits (F), power nailer (G).

Power & Pneumatic Tools

Outdoor building projects and landscaping work often require the use of power tools and specialty tools. Home centers will have the common power tools you will require, but if your project demands a tool that you will only use once or that is expensive, consider renting it.

Pneumatic tools are increasingly popular for use by the do-it-yourselfer Pneumatic tools are not confined to the basic air framing-nail gun or finish-nail gun. Air hammers, or pneumatic chisels, are a good tool to consider purchasing if you own a compressor. They take the work out of splitting pavers and stone with a manual hammer and a cold chisel.

To ensure your safety, always use a ground-fault circuit interrupter (GFCI) extension cord, and wear protective gear, such as work glasses, particle masks, and work gloves.

Rental Tools

When power tools are expensive or you only need them for one-time use, consider renting. Rental centers have a large selection of tools available from small tools like jig saws to large heavy equipment like end loaders and spreaders.

Many home centers now have smaller, convenient in-store rental equipment available.

If your project requires moving large amounts of material, or grading an area too big to do by hand, check with your local rental center outlet for bigger equipment rental. These machines are generally available for longer periods of time and may include instructional information sessions for proper use.

Use rental equipment safely, making sure you are familiar with proper usage and operation of each tool. Read owner's manuals and all safety instructions to prevent damage to tools and to prevent personal injury.

Pneumatic tools include: air compressor (A), air hose (B), framing-nail gun (C), finish-nail gun (D), air hammer with chisel bits (E).

A front-end loader is useful if you need to move large amounts of material. Front-end loaders are available for daily or long-term rental.

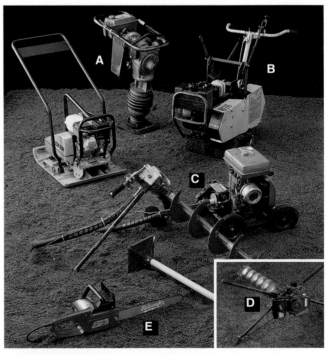

Specialty tools you can rent include: tamping machines (A), sod cutter (B), power auger (C), two-person power auger (D), chain saw (E).

Codes & Considerations

For almost any building project, there are local regulations you should consider. Building codes, zoning ordinances, and permits are the legal issues you'll have to contend with, but you should also consider how your project will fit into the neighborhood and the effect it will have on your neighbors.

Building codes exist to ensure that the materials and construction methods of your project are safe. Zoning laws govern the size, location, and style of your structure to preserve aesthetic standards. Permits and inspections are required to ensure your plans meet all local building and zoning restrictions.

Requirements and restrictions vary from one community to the next, so make sure to check the codes for your area. If your plans conflict with local codes, you may be able to apply for a variance, which allows you to bypass the strict requirements of the code. In some cases, you'll need the agreement of your neighbors in order to obtain a variance.

Talk to your local building inspection department early to determine if your project requires a permit and whether you must submit plans for approval. The permit process can take several weeks or months, so checking early helps avoid delays. Fill out the necessary forms, pay any applicable fees, and wait for your approval

Discuss your plans with neighbors as well. A fence, wall, or gate on or near a property line is as much a part of your neighbors' landscapes as your own. The tall hedge you've planned for privacy may cast a dense shadow over your neighbor's sunbathing deck. The simple courtesy of letting your neighbors know what you're planning can keep everyone on a friendly basis, and can even help avoid legal disputes.

You may find that discussing your plans with neighbors reaps unexpected rewards. You and your neighbor may decide to share labor and expenses by landscaping both properties at once. Or you may combine resources on a key feature that benefits both yards, such as a stone garden wall or shade tree.

In addition, check with your local utility companies to pinpoint the locations of any underground electrical, plumbing, sewer, or telephone lines on your property. These locations can have an impact on your plans if your project requires digging or changes to your property's grade. There is no charge to have utility companies locate these lines, and it can prevent you from making an expensive or life-threatening mistake. In many areas, the law requires that you have this done before digging any holes.

On the following pages, you'll find some common legal restrictions for typical landscape projects.

Fences

- Height: The maximum height of a fence may be restricted by your local building code. In some communities, backyard fences are limited to 6 ft. in height, while front yard fences are limited to 3 ft. or 4 ft.—or prohibited altogether.

- Setback: Even if not specified by your building code, it's a good idea to position your fence 12" or so inside the official property line to avoid any possible boundary disputes. Correspondingly, don't assume that a neighbor's fence marks the exact boundary of your property. For example, before digging an elaborate planting bed up to the edge of your neighbor's fence, it's best to make sure you're not encroaching on someone else's land.

- Gates: Gates must be at least 3 ft. wide. If you plan to push a wheelbarrow through it, your gate width should be 4 ft.

Driveways

- Width: Straight driveways should be at least 10 ft. wide; 12 ft. is better. On sharp curves, the driveway should be 14 ft. wide.

- Thickness: Concrete driveways should be at least 6" thick.

- Base: Because it must tolerate considerable weight, a concrete or brick paver driveway should have a compactible gravel base that is at least 6" thick.

- Drainage: A driveway should slope ¼" per foot away from a house or garage. The center of the driveway should be crowned so it is 1" higher in the center than on the sides.

- Reinforcement: Your local building code probably requires that all concrete driveways be reinforced with iron rebar or steel mesh for strength

Sidewalks & Paths

- Size of sidewalks: Traditional concrete sidewalks should be 4 ft. to 5 ft. wide to allow two people to comfortably pass one another, and 3" to 4" thick.

- Width of garden paths: Informal pathways may be 2 ft. to 3 ft. wide, although stepping-stone pathways can be even narrower.

- Base: Most building codes require that a concrete or brick side walk be laid on a base of compactible gravel at least 4" thick. Standard concrete sidewalks may also need to be reinforced with iron rebar or steel mesh for strength

- Surface & drainage: Concrete sidewalk surfaces should be textured to provide a nonslip surface, and crowned or slanted ¼" per foot to ensure that water doesn't puddle.

- Sand-set paver walkways: Brick pavers should be laid on a 3"-thick base of sand.

Fences should be set back at least 1 ft. from the formal property lines.

Driveways should be at least 10 ft. wide to accommodate vehicles.

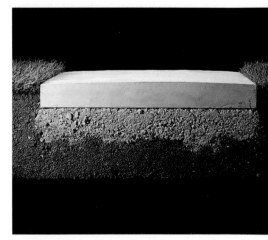

Concrete paving should be laid on a bed of gravel to provide drainage.

(continued next page)

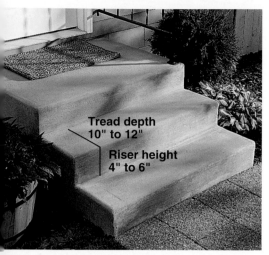

Concrete steps should use a comfortable tread depth and riser height.

Concrete patios require reinforcement with steel mesh or rebar.

Mortared garden walls need to be supported by concrete footings.

Steps

- Proportion of riser to tread depth: In general, steps should be proportioned so that the sum of the depth, plus the riser multiplied by two, is between 25" and 27". A 15" depth and 6" rise, for example, is a comfortable step (15 + 12 = 27); as is an 18" depth and 4" rise (18 + 8 = 26).

- Railings: Building codes may require railings for any stairway with more than three steps, especially for stairs that lead to an entrance to your home.

Concrete Patios

- Base: Concrete patios should have a subbase of compactible gravel at least 4" thick. Concrete slabs for patios should be at least 3" thick.

- Reinforcement: Concrete slabs should be reinforced with wire mesh or a grid of rebar.

Garden Walls

- Footings: Mortared brick or stone garden walls more than 4 ft. in height often require concrete footings that extend below the winter frost line. Failure to follow this regulation can result in a hefty fine or a demolition order, as well as a flimsy, dangerous wall.

- Drainage: Dry-set stone garden walls installed without concrete footings should have a base of compactible gravel at least 6" thick to ensure the stability of the wall.

Swimming Pools

- Fences: Nearly all building codes require a protective fence around swimming pools to keep young children and animals away from the water.

- Location: In some areas, building codes require that below-ground swimming pools be at least 10 ft. away from a building foundation.

Retaining Walls

- Height: For do-it-yourself construction, retaining walls should be no more than 4 ft. high. Higher slopes should be terraced with two or more short retaining walls.

- Batter: A retaining wall should have a backward slant (batter) of 2" to 3" for dry-set stones; 1" to 2" for mortared stones.

- Footings: Retaining walls higher than 4 ft. must have concrete footings that extend down below the frost line. This helps ensure the stability of the wall.

Ponds

- Safety: To ensure child safety, some communities restrict land scape ponds to a depth of 12" to 18", unless surrounded by a protective fence or covered with heavy wire mesh.

Decks

- Structural members: Determining the proper spacing and size for structural elements of a deck can be a complicated process, but if you follow these guidelines, you will satisfy code require ments in most areas:

BEAM SIZE & SPAN

Beam size	Maximum spacing between posts
two 2 x 8s	8 ft.
two 2 x 10s	10 ft.
two 2 x 12s	12 ft.

JOIST SIZE & SPAN

Joist size	Maximum distance between beams (Joists 16" apart)
2 x 6	8 ft.
2 x 8	10 ft.
2 x 10	13 ft.

- Decking boards: Surface decking boards should be spaced so the gaps between boards are no more than ¼" wide.
- Railings: Any deck more than 24" high requires a railing. Gaps between rails or balusters should be no more than 4".
- Post footings: Concrete footings should be at least 8" in diameter If a deck is attached to a permanent structure, the footings must extend below the frost line in your region.

Sheds

- Setback: Most zoning laws require that outbuildings must be set back a specific distance from property lines. Depending on your community, the distance could be as little as 6" or as much as 3 ft. or more.
- Building permits: Often required if shed has wiring and plumbing or if it exceeds a maximum size defined as a temporary structure.

A series of short retaining walls, rather than one tall wall, is the best way to handle a slope.

Railing balusters are required by building code to be spaced no more than 4" apart to keep small children from slipping through or being trapped between them.

Sheds larger than 120 square feet may require a permit, but temporary structures typically do not.

Drawing Plans

Not every landscape project requires a detailed plan drawing, but the more steps involved in a project, the more likely it is that plan drawings will help you organize your work. In addition to having working plans for each project, it's a good idea to develop an overall plan for your entire landscape. Working with a master plan can prevent the haphazard look that sometimes occurs when a landscape evolves without good planning.

With that in mind, the following few pages will show a simple method for creating an overall landscaping plan, as well as for creating working plan drawings for specific projects. It's not important that your drawings be great works of art; what is important is that they give you a way to visualize your finished landscape and specific projects in that landscape. Some plan drawings that are little more than sketches are completely serviceable for landscape planning.

Creating plans for a landscape includes these steps: • Surveying your yard ; • Drawing a site map; • Sketching bubble plans; • Creating a landscape design • Creating working drawings

1. Surveying Your Yard

Measuring your yard doesn't have to be done with precise surveying equipment, but it is very helpful to spend some time with a tape measure before you begin drawing plans. These measurements provide the information you need to create all other landscape drawings. Good measurements are also essential for projects where building permits are required.

Make a rough sketch of your yard, then make measurements that are as accurate as possible. Some landscape projects require digging, so contact your local utility companies to mark the locations of any underground power, gas, or communications lines. If the property boundaries aren't clear, you may also need to contact your county surveyor's office to come and mark the precise boundary lines for you. This can be very important if your landscaping plans will include a fence or garden wall that adjoins the property line.

Straight lines and square corners are easy enough to measure and mark, but it can be a bit harder to precisely locate features that have irregular

How to Make a Yard Survey

1 Measure the position of all the features of your yard, relative to the property lines. This work may require a helper and a long tape measure.

2 Use the survey measurements to create a rough drawing of your yard.

shapes, or features that are angled in relation to the main property lines. In this case, you can use a method called triangulation to determine precise positions. On a square lot, for example, you can determine the location of a large tree most accurately by measuring the distance to the tree from two corners of the property.

On a yard with significant slopes, make cross-section drawings, called elevations, to indicate the vertical rise of the landscape. Elevations are drawings that show the landscape as viewed from the side. They'll be important for planning fence, garden wall, or retaining wall projects.

2. Drawing a Site Map

Using your survey measurements and the rough sketch, you'll now create a more accurate and precise drawing of your yard, called a site map. This is nothing more than a drawing that shows the basic permanent features of your yard. It will include the property lines and all buildings on the site, as well as other permanent structures, like driveways or large trees.

The site map is an overhead view of your yard, drawn to scale. It is the basis for the finished landscape design.

A scale of 1/8" = 1 ft. is a good scale to use for site maps and landscape plans. At this scale, you can map a yard as big as 60 x 80 ft. on a standard sheet of paper, or an 80 x 130-ft. yard on a 11 x 17" sheet of paper. If your yard is bigger than this, you can tape several sheets together.

Decimal Equivalents:

Converting actual measurements often produces decimal fractions, which then must be converted to ruler measurements. Use this chart to determine equivalents.

Decimal	Fraction	Decimal	Fraction
.0625	1/16	.5625	9/16
.125	1/8	.625	5/8
.1875	3/16	.6875	11/16
.25	1/4	.75	3/4
.3125	5/16	.8125	13/16
.375	3/8	.875	7/8
.4375	7/16	.9375	15/16
.5	1/2		

How to Draw a Site Map

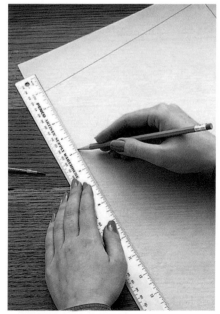

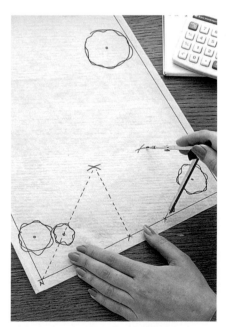

1 Convert all the measurements you made in the survey to scale measurements. Then outline your yard by drawing the straight boundaries to scale.

2 Where you triangulated measurements from property corners, set a compass to the scale measurements, then draw arcs on the drawing. Where the arcs intersect is the precise location of the triangulated measurements.

3 Use a plastic triangle and ruler to mark the edges and corners of all structures within the boundaries of your yard.

3. Sketching Bubble Plans

Bubble plans are rough sketches in which you play with different ideas for arranging features within your overall yard. They are a great way to test out different ideas before committing to them. You might, for example, draw your yard with a patio positioned in different locations to see how it feels in relationship to your deck and garden beds.

Draw lots of variations of your ideas, and feel free to play with ideas that seem a little extreme. Professional designers sometimes go through dozens of ideas before settling on one that will eventually turn into a final landscape design.

The place to start is with lots of photocopies of the site map you've created. Or, you can use tracing paper to play with bubble plan ideas. Tracing paper is available at art supply stores.

Make sure to include the other members of your household in this important planning step. They'll be enthusiastic about the work if you've included everyone in the planning process.

4. Creating a Landscape Design

Once your bubble plan experiments have yielded a plan you like, it's time to turn it into a formal landscape design. The landscape design will serve as a road map for your future landscape. It's particularly helpful if you have a big landscape renovation planned that will take several seasons to complete.

The landcape design can be a chance to have some artistic fun. You can illustrate your design in color, if you want. You may have a few false starts, so it will help to have several copies of your final site map when you begin.

The key to a professional-looking design is to use smooth flowing lines rather than straight lines and sharp angles. Aim for a feeling of continuous flow through the different areas of your landscape. In the final design, the boundaries of the spaces should resemble the rounded flowing lines of your bubble plan.

5. Creating Working Drawings

The final step of this planning process is the

How to Sketch Bubble Plans

1 Sketch the landscape features you're considering on a photocopy or tracing paper copy of your site map. Feel free to experiment; it costs nothing to dream.

2 You can test different bubble plans in your yard by outlining features with stakes and string. You can use cardboard cutouts to represent stepping-stones and walkways.

starting point for the actual projects you'll find on the pages of this book. Working drawings are individual plans for specific projects within your overall landscape. If you happen to be working from a pre-existing plan, such as a deck or gazebo blueprint, you may not need to make your own drawings. If you're designing your own project, though, making working drawings is what will let you estimate materials and organize your steps.

Working plans serve the same function for landscape construction as blueprints do for builders creating a house. The working plan is a bare-bones version of a plan drawing that includes only the measurements and specifications needed to actually create the project.

How to Create a Landscape Design

1 On a fresh copy of your site map, outline the hardscape features, including patio or deck surfaces, fences, walls, hedges, garden areas, and pathways.

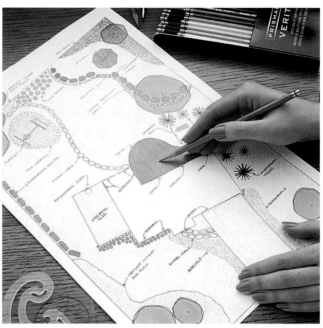

2 Add symbols and textures for any remaining elements, then use colored pencils to finish the design.

How to Create Working Drawings

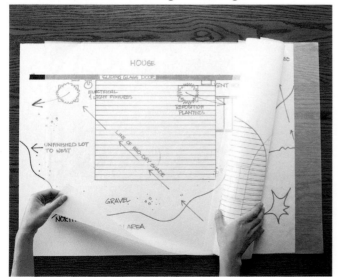

1 On an enlargment of your landscape design, or using tracing paper, make a more detailed overhead view of the specific project, showing structural measurements

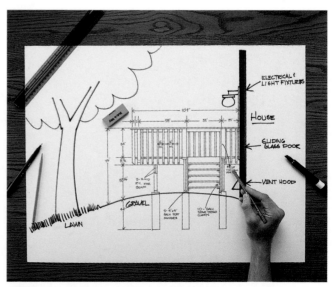

2 Create detailed plan and elevation drawings for your project. List all dimensions on the drawing, and indicate size, type, and quantities of lumber and hardware needed.

Shaping Your Yard

Newly constructed homes are often left with yards that are flat as the proverbial pool table, and many stay this way for decades. Flat landscapes not only are visually unappealing, but they can be subject to drainage problems that can create basement water problems or boggy areas where grass or ground covers have trouble thriving. Another common problem is a yard with a steep slope that is hard to maintain and isn't practical for recreational use.

The projects in this section give solutions to these problems. If you're lanscaping a newly constructed home, then you have the advantage of doing this work before the problems have developed. If you have an established landscape, now's your chance to solve long-standing problems.

If you have a flat yard, you'll learn how to create visual contours by adding a landscape berm. If you have problematic slopes, you'll learn how to create flat terraces with retaining walls. If you have drainage problems, you'll learn a variety of solutions for eliminating them.

These are major yard-shaping projects that should be addressed before you get to the more decorative landscaping projects found elsewhere in this book. Building a new patio, for example, might be wasted effort if you haven't addressed the drainage problems in your yard.

These projects can entail moving a considerable amount of earth. There is no reason you can't do this by hand if you take your time. But for faster results, you can also rent a small motorized front-loader or hire an earth-moving contractor to haul in additional earth or move existing earth around.

• **Building a berm** (page 32).

• **Grading your yard** (page 34).

• **Building a swale or dry creek** (page 36).
• **Installing a dry well** (page 38).

• **Building terrraces** (page 40).

Building a Berm

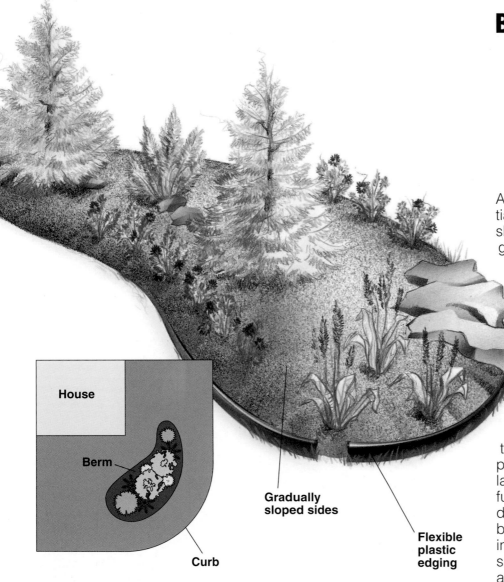

House

Berm

Curb

Gradually sloped sides

Flexible plastic edging

A landscape berm is essentially a small hill with a gentle slope. Whether planted with grass or used as a planting area as shown here, a berm will add visual appeal to a flat yard, and can be used to screen out unpleasant views. It can even absorb some of the noise from nearby traffic.

The most attractive examples have gentle slopes and irregular shapes that accent the surrounding yard. If you're planning to construct a particularly high or wide berm, carefully position it so that water drains efficiently. And don't build a berm around an existing tree. You can very easily smother a tree's root system and kill it.

Since building a berm involves creating an elevated area, you'll undoubtedly need to add soil. Before using soil from another area of the yard, collect samples and have a soil test conducted to make sure the soil is capable of supporting trees and plants. You may be better off purchasing high-grade topsoil from a soil contractor and having it delivered.

Edging Materials

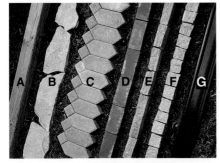

A variety of edging materials is available. Look for ways to repeat existing materials in your landscape. Here are a few commonly used options:

A. Cut timbers can be used as edging on straight garden beds.

B. Flagstones are relatively inexpensive. Their rough texture works well in informal, country, or cottage-style landscapes.

C. Geometric pavers make an attractive, durable edging.

D. Bricks are a traditional material used in formal-looking landscapes. They can be arranged end to end, side by side, or even upright for a slightly raised edging.

E. Concrete rubble scavenged from demolition sites can be laid broken side up to make an inexpensive, textured edging.

F. Cut stones (called ashlars) are a premium building material that lends a unique, tailored look to berms.

G. Plastic landscape edging can be purchased at landscape and gardening centers.

Everything You Need

Tools: Basic tools (page 18), flexible plastic edging, stakes, hand tamp.

Materials: Plantings, mulch.

How to Build a Berm

1 Using a hose or rope, create an outline for the planned berm. Using a spade, remove all grass or ground cover growing inside the outline. If the berm is large, you may want to use a sod cutter.

2 With a trenching spade, dig a trench around the perimeter of the berm area, just wide enough to install the flexible plastic edging. To hold the edging in place, use a maul to drive stakes through the bottom lip of the edging.

3 Fill the outlined area with topsoil. Using a garden rake, distribute the soil so that the berm is 18" to 24" tall at the highest point. When all the necessary soil is added, grade the sides into a gradual slope. Using a hand tamp, compact the entire surface of the berm, then water the soil to further compress it.

4 Plant trees, shrubs, or other plants in the berm. Apply a 2" to 3" layer of mulch over the surface of the berm to prevent weeds and retain moisture.

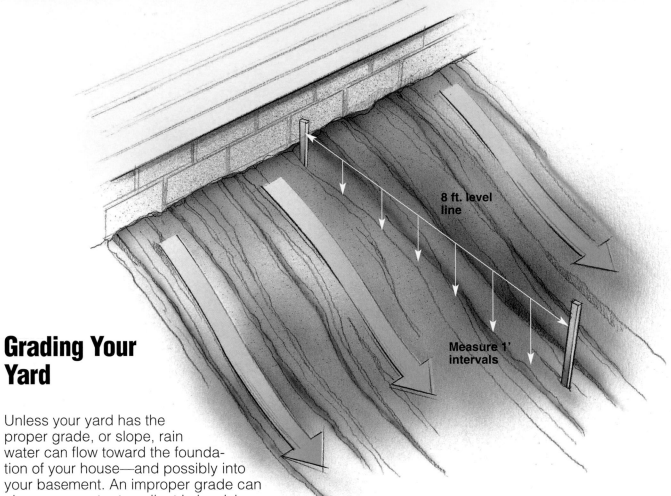

8 ft. level line

Measure 1' intervals

Grading Your Yard

Unless your yard has the proper grade, or slope, rain water can flow toward the foundation of your house—and possibly into your basement. An improper grade can also cause water to collect in low-lying areas, creating boggy spots where you'll have trouble growing grass and other plants. When graded correctly, your yard should have a gradual slope away from the house of about ¾" per horizontal foot.

Although the initial grading of a yard is usually done by a landscape contractor, you can do the work yourself to save money. The job is a bit time-consuming, but it isn't difficult. Typically, creating a grade at this stage involves spreading a 4" to 6" layer of topsoil over the yard, then distributing and smoothing it to slope away from the house.

Established landscapes often require regrading, especially if the house has settled. If you find signs of basement moisture problems or puddle-prone areas in the yard, you need to correct the slope. The measuring and grading techniques featured here will help you remove and distribute soil as needed.

Everything You Need

Tools: Basic tools (page 18), line level, grading rake, stakes, string, tape, hand tamp.

Materials: Topsoil.

How to Measure & Establish a Grade

1 Drive a stake into the soil at the base of the foundation and another at least 8 ft. out into the yard along a straight line from the first stake. Attach a string fitted with a line level to the stakes and level it. Measure and flag the string with tape at 1-ft. intervals. Measure down from the string at the tape flags, recording your measurements to use as guidelines for adding or removing soil to create a correct grade.

2 Working away from the base of the house, add soil to low areas until they reach the desired height. Using a garden rake, evenly distribute the soil over a small area. Measure down from the 1-ft. markings as you work to make sure that you are creating a ¾" per 1 ft. pitch. Add and remove soil as needed until soil is evenly sloped, then move on to the next area and repeat the process.

3 Use a hand tamp to lightly compact the soil. Don't over-tamp the soil or it could become too dense to grow a healthy lawn or plants.

4 After all the soil is tamped, use a grading rake to remove any rocks or clumps. Starting at the foundation, pull the rake in a straight line down the slope. Dispose of any rocks or construction debris. Repeat the process, working on one section at a time until the entire area around the house is graded.

Variation: You may want to create some perfectly level areas for playing lawn sports such as croquet, badminton, volleyball, and lawn bowling. Level areas also make safe play surfaces for small children and a good base for play structures.

Outline the perimeter of the area with evenly placed stakes. Extend a string fitted with a line level between a pair of stakes and adjust the string until it's level. At 2-ft. intervals, measure down from the marked areas of the string to the ground.

Add and remove topsoil as necessary, distributing it with a garden rake until the surface under the string is level. Repeat the process until the entire area is leveled.

Installing a Dry Well

A dry well is a simple method for channeling excess water out of low-lying or water-laden areas, such as the ground beneath a gutter downspout. A dry well system typically consists of a buried drain tile running from a catch basin positioned at the problem spot to a collection container some distance away.

A dry well system is easy to install and surprisingly inexpensive. In the project shown here, a perforated plastic drain tile carries water from a catch basin to a dry well fashioned from a plastic trash can, which has been punctured, then filled with stone rubble. The runoff water percolates into the soil as it makes its way along the drain pipe and through the dry well.

The how-to steps of this project include digging the trench with a shovel. If the catch basin is a long distance from the problem area, you may want to rent a trencher to dig the trench quickly. Call local utility companies to mark the location of underground mechanicals before you start to dig.

Everything You Need:

Tools: Stakes, string, line level, trench spade, power tools (page 20), trencher (optional)

Materials: Sod, landscape fabric, gravel and large stones, drain tile, plastic trash can

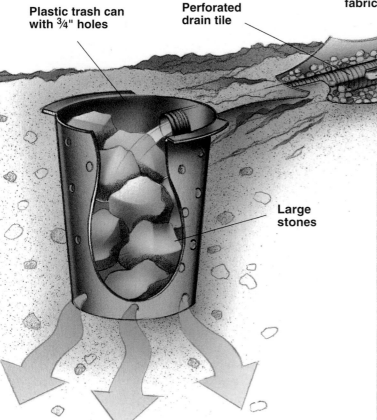

Plastic trash can with ¾" holes

Perforated drain tile

Landscape fabric

Catch basin

Gravel

Large stones

How to Install a Dry Well

1 Use stakes to mark a path from the problem area to the catch basin. Dig a 10"-wide, 14"-deep trench along the route from the catch basin to the dry well. Slope the trench 2" for every 8ft. of length. Dig a hole for the dry well container 4" larger than the bucket's dimensions.

2 Line the hole and trench with landscape fabric. Fold the excess over the sides of the trench and hole. Lay a 1" layer of gravel on the bottom of the trench. Place the drain tile in the trench. Trace the outline of the drain tile 3" from the top of the trash can. Cut a hole along the outline using a jig saw.

3 Use a drill with a 1" bit to drill drainage holes through the sides and bottom of the can every 4" to 6". Place the can in the hole, run the drain tile 2" into the side of the can, and fill the can with large rocks, flattening them at the top. Fold the landscape fabric over the rocks. Fill the hole with soil.

4 Check the slope of the drain tile with a level, adjusting the layer of gravel below if necessary. Connect the catch basin in the problem area. Position it so the excess water will flow directly into it. Fill the trench with gravel, 1" over the drain tile.

5 Fold the edges of the landscape fabric over the gravel-covered drain tile and fill the trench with the soil you removed earlier. Replace the sod in the trench area. Tamp it lightly with a shovel. Water the area thoroughly.

How to Prepare a Retaining Wall Site

1 Excavate the hillside if necessary to create a level base for the retaining wall. For interlocking blocks or stone walls, allow at least 12" of space for gravel backfill between the back of the wall and the hillside. For timber wails, allow at least 3 ft. of space. When excavating large areas, rent earth-moving equipment or hire a contractor.

2 Use stakes to mark the front edge of the wall at the ends and at any corners and curves. Connect the stakes with mason's string. Use a line level to check the string, and if necessary adjust the string so it is level.

3 Dig a trench for the first row of building materials, measuring down from the mason's string to maintain a level trench. Make the trench 6" deeper than the thickness of one layer of building material. For example, if you are using 6"-thick interlocking clocks, make the trench 12" deep.

4 Line the excavation with strips of landscape fabric cut 3 ft. longer than the planned height of the wall. Make sure seams overlap by at least 6".

How to Build a Natural Stone Retaining Wall

Retaining walls made from natural cut stone give a traditional, timeless look to a landscape. Natural stone walls are usually laid out without mortar, although the last two rows can be mortared in place for greater strength.

Before building the wall, prepare the site as directed on page 40. Build the wall by placing the largest stones at the bottom and reserving the smoothest flattest stones for the corners and cap row.

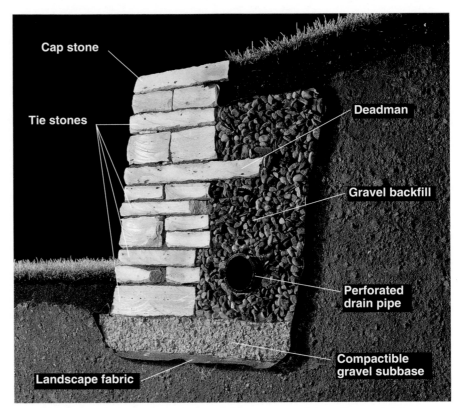

Cut stone has flat, smooth surfaces for easy stacking. For a stable retaining wall, alternate rows of "tie stones" that span the entire width of the wall with rows of smaller stones. Install extra-long stones (called deadmen) that extend back into gravel backfill, spaced every 4 to 6 ft.

Trim irregular stones if needed to make them fit solidly into the wall. Always wear eye protection and hearing protectors when cutting stone. Score the stone first using a masonry blade and circular saw set to ⅛" blade depth, then drive a masonry chisel along the scored line until the stone breaks.

1 Spread a 6" layer of compactible gravel subbase into the prepared trench (step 1, page 46), then sort the stones by size and shape so they can be located easily as you build. Make sure you have enough long stones to serve as tie stones, deadmen, and capstones.

(continued next page)

2 Lay rows of stones, following the same techniques for backfilling as for interlocking blocks (page 46). Build a backward slant (batter) into the wall by setting each row of stones about ½" back from the preceding row. For stability, work tie stones and deadmen into the wall at frequent intervals.

3 Before laying the cap row of stones, mix mortar according to the manufacturer's directions and apply a thick bed along the tops of the installed stones, keeping the mortar 6" from the front face of the wall. Lay the capstones and press them into the mortar. Finish backfilling behind the wall and in the trench at the base of the wall with topsoil. Install sod or other plants as desired.

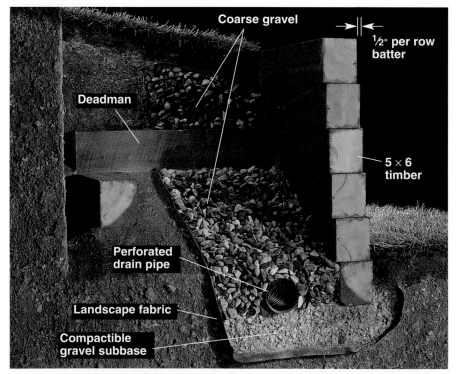

Timber retaining walls must be anchored with deadmen that extend from the wall back into the soil. Deadmen prevent the wall from sagging under the weight of the soil. For best results with timber retaining walls, create a backward angle (batter) by setting each row of timbers ½" behind the preceding row. The first row of timbers should be buried.

Building a Retaining Wall Using Timbers

Timber walls have a lifespan of 15 to 20 years if built correctly. If you are interested in the look of timber walls but would like a longer wall life consider using a composite timber (page 10).

Use a chain saw or reciprocating saw to cut timbers. Avoid using old timbers, like discarded railroad ties that have been soaked in creosote. Creosote can leach into the soil and kill plants or contaminate groundwater.

Before building the retaining wall, prepare the site as directed on page 42.

44

How To Build a Wood Timber Retaining Wall

1 Spread a 6" layer of compactible gravel into the prepared trench. Tamp it thoroughly and begin laying timbers following the techniques for interlocking blocks on page 46. Each row should be set with a ½" batter. End joints should be staggered.

2 Use 12" galvanized spikes or reinforcement bars to anchor the ends of each timber to the underlying timbers. Stagger the ends to form strong corner joints. Drive spikes along the length of the timbers at 2-ft. intervals. If necessary, drill pilot holes.

3 Install deadmen. spaced 4 ft. apart, midway up the wall. Build the deadmen by joining 3-ft.-long lengths of timber with 12" spikes, then insert the ends through holes cut in the landscape fabric. Anchor deadmen to wall with spikes. Install the remaining rows of timbers, and finish backfilling behind the wall.

4 Improve drainage by drilling weep holes through the second row of landscape timbers and into the gravel backfill, using a spade bit. Space the holes 4 ft. apart, and angle them upward.

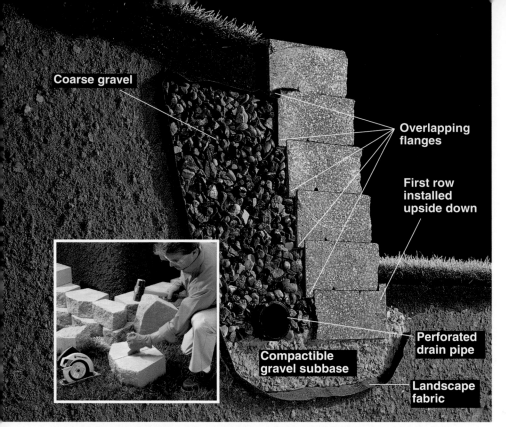

Coarse gravel

Overlapping flanges

First row installed upside down

Perforated drain pipe

Compactible gravel subbase

Landscape fabric

Building a Terrace with Interlocking Block

Several styles of interlocking block are available at building and outdoor centers. Most types have a natural rock finish that combines the rough texture of cut stone with the uniform shape and size of concrete blocks.

Interlocking blocks weigh up to 80 lb. each, so it is a good idea to have helpers when building a retaining wall. Suppliers offer substantial discounts when interlocking block is purchased in large quantities, so you may be able to save money if you coordinate your own project with those of your neighbors.

Interlocking blocks do not need mortar. Some types are held together with a system of overlapping flanges. Make half blocks for corners by scoring full blocks with a circular saw and masonry blade. Break the blocks along the score with a maul and chisel.

How to Build a Terrrace with Interlocking Block

1 Spread a 6" layer of compactible gravel into the trench and pack thoroughly. A rented tamping machine works better than a hand tamper. Lay the first row of blocks, aligning the front edge with the mason's string. If using flanged blocks, place the first row upside down and backward. Check the blocks with a level, adjusting if necessary.

2 Lay the second course of blocks following the manufacturer's instructions. Check the blocks frequently to make sure they are level. Add 6" of gravel behind the blocks, making sure the landscape fabric remains between the gravel and the hillside. Pack the gravel thoroughly with a hand tamper.

3 Place perforated drainpipe on top of the gravel, at least 6" behind the wall, with perforations facing down. Make sure that at least one end of the pipe is unobstructed so runoff water can escape. Lay additional rows of blocks until the wall is about 18" above ground level. Make sure the vertical joints in adjoining walls are offset.

4 Fill behind the wall with coarse gravel, and pack well. Lay the remaining rows of block, except for the cap row, backfilling with gravel and packing with a hand tamper as you go.

5 Before laying the cap blocks, fold the end of the landscape fabric over the gravel backfill. Add a thin layer of topsoil over the fabric, then pack it thoroughly with a hand tamper.

6 Fold any excess landscape fabric back over the soil, then apply construction adhesive to the blocks. Lay the cap blocks in place. Use topsoil to fill in behind the wall and to fill in the trench at the base of the wall. Install sod or other plants, as desired.

Electricity & Water

To be fully functional, a landscape requires electrical service and plumbing lines, just like your home. Electrical service can range from a simple receptacle outlet mounted on your home's exterior, to multiple electrical circuits bringing power to lighting systems and other accessories. Plumbing will usually include at least one hose spigot for basic watering, but a more full-featured landscape may have an underground sprinkler system, an outdoor sink, or even a shower.

Adding or expanding your landscape's wiring and plumbing service can make your yard a truly functional space, suitable for any purpose.

You should have some knowledge of basic wiring and plumbing, as well as experience doing projects like these before tacklilng the projects in this section. Always contact your local building inspections office to find out if permits and inspections are required for the work you're planning.

- **Installing an outdoor electrical circuit** (page 50).

- **Circuit variation: lamp post** (page 62).

- **Installing low-voltage lighting** (page 64).

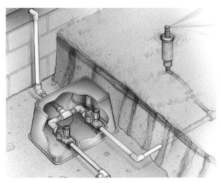
- **Installing an in-ground sprinkler system** (page 68).

- **Installing a drip irrigation system** (page 72).

- **Installing a rain barrel irrigation system** (page 74).

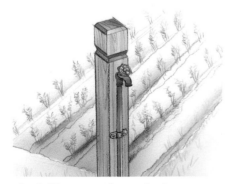
- **Installing a garden spigot** (page 76).

- **Installing an outdoor sink** (page 78).

- **Installing an outdoor shower** (page 80).

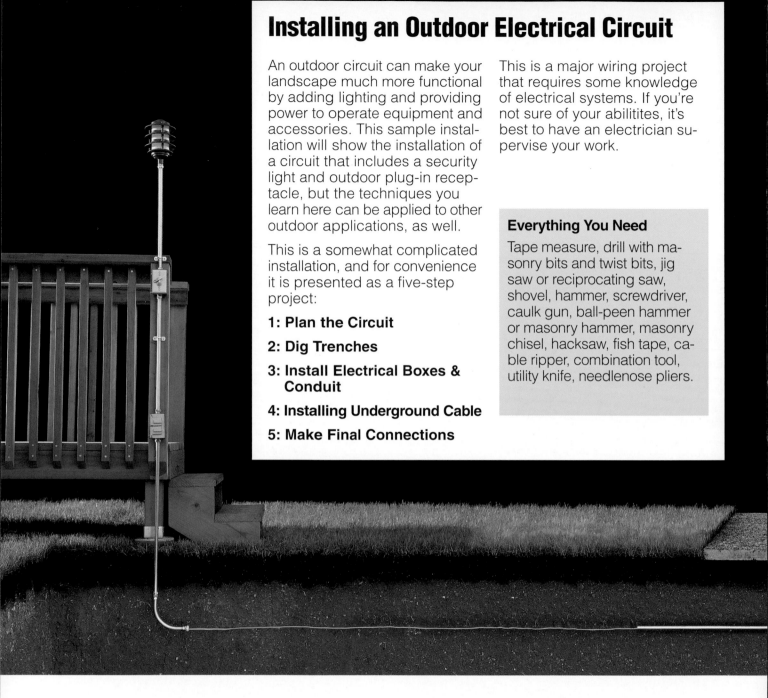

Installing an Outdoor Electrical Circuit

An outdoor circuit can make your landscape much more functional by adding lighting and providing power to operate equipment and accessories. This sample installation will show the installation of a circuit that includes a security light and outdoor plug-in receptacle, but the techniques you learn here can be applied to other outdoor applications, as well.

This is a somewhat complicated installation, and for convenience it is presented as a five-step project:

1: Plan the Circuit

2: Dig Trenches

3: Install Electrical Boxes & Conduit

4: Installing Underground Cable

5: Make Final Connections

This is a major wiring project that requires some knowledge of electrical systems. If you're not sure of your abilitites, it's best to have an electrician supervise your work.

Everything You Need

Tape measure, drill with masonry bits and twist bits, jig saw or reciprocating saw, shovel, hammer, screwdriver, caulk gun, ball-peen hammer or masonry hammer, masonry chisel, hacksaw, fish tape, cable ripper, combination tool, utility knife, needlenose pliers.

1: Plan the Circuit

As you begin planning an outdoor circuit, visit your electrical inspector to learn about local code requirements for outdoor wiring. The techniques for installing outdoor circuits are much the same as for installing indoor wiring. However, because outdoor wiring is exposed to the elements, it requires the use of special weatherproof materials, including underground feeder (UF) cable, rigid metal or schedule 40 PVC plastic conduit, and weatherproof electrical boxes and fittings.

Because climate and soil conditions vary from region to region, your local building and electrical codes may have special requirements. For example, some regions require that all underground cables be protected with conduit, while in other areas you can bury special UF cable without protection.

Most homes don't require a lot of power for outdoor needs. Adding a new 15-amp, 120-volt circuit is usually enough. However, if your circuit will include more than three large light fixtures (each rated for 300 watts or more) or more than

Check for underground utilities when planning trenches. Avoid lawn sprinkler pipes, and consult your electric utility office, phone company, gas and water department, and cable television vendor for the exact locations of underground utility lines. Many utility companies send field representatives to show homeowners how to avoid dangerous underground hazards.

Choosing Cable Sizes for an Outdoor Circuit

Circuit length		
Less than 50 ft.	50 ft. or more	Circuit size
14-gauge	12-gauge	15-amp
12-gauge	10-gauge	20-amp

Consider the circuit length when choosing cable sizes for an outdoor circuit. In very long circuits, normal wire resistance leads to a substantial drop in voltage. If your outdoor circuit extends more than 50 ft., use larger-gauge wire to reduce the voltage drop. For example, a 15-amp circuit that extends more than 50 ft. should be wired with 12-gauge wire instead of 14-gauge. A 20-amp circuit longer than 50 ft. should be wired with 10-gauge cable.

four receptacles, plan to install a 20-amp, 120-volt circuit. Or, if you'll also be heating a hot tub or other heating appliance, you may require several 120-volt and 240-volt circuits.

A typical outdoor circuit takes one or two weekends to install, but if your layout requires very long lengths of underground cables, allow yourself more time for digging trenches, or arrange to have extra help. Also make sure to allow time for the required inspection visits when planning your wiring project.

Tips for Planning an Outdoor Circuit

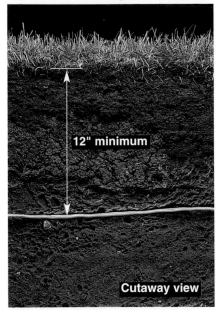

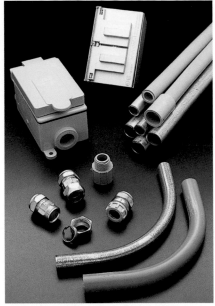

Bury UF cables 12" deep if the wires are protected by a GFCI and the circuit is no larger than 20 amps. Bury cable at least 18" deep if the circuit is not protected by a GFCI or if it is larger than 20 amps.

Protect cable entering conduit by attaching a plastic bushing to the open end of the conduit. The bushing prevents sharp metal edges from damaging the vinyl sheathing on the cable.

Protect exposed wiring above ground level with rigid conduit and weatherproof electrical boxes and coverplates. Check your local code restrictions: some regions allow the use of either rigid metal conduit or schedule 40 PVC plastic conduit and electrical boxes, while other regions allow only metal.

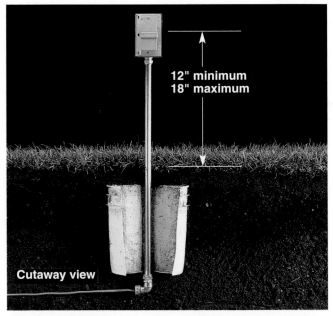

Prevent shock by making sure all outdoor receptacles are protected by a ground-fault circuit-interrupter (GFCI) receptacle. A single GFCI receptacle can be wired to protect other fixtures on the circuit. Outdoor receptacles should be at least 1 foot above ground level and enclosed in weatherproof electrical boxes with watertight covers.

Anchor freestanding receptacles that are not attached to a structure by embedding the rigid metal conduit or schedule 40 PVC plastic conduit in a concrete footing. One way to do this is by running conduit through a plastic bucket, then filling the bucket with concrete. Freestanding receptacles should be at least 12", but no more than 18", above ground level—requirements vary, so check with your local inspector.

2: Dig Trenches

Outdoor circuits require that you run cables underground. To save time and minimize lawn damage, plan circuit routes to reduce the length of cable runs, and make your trenches as narrow as possible.

If your soil is sandy, or very hard and dry, water the ground thoroughly before you begin digging. Lawn sod can be removed, set on strips of plastic, and replaced after cables are laid. Keep the removed sod moist but not wet, and replace it within two or three days. Otherwise, the grass underneath the plastic may die.

If trenches must be left unattended, make sure to cover them with scrap pieces of plywood to prevent accidents and to keep water out.

Everything You Need

Stakes, string, scrap piece of conduit, compression fittings, plastic bushings.

1 Mark the outline of trenches with wooden stakes and string.

2 Cut two 18"-wide strips of plastic, and place one strip on each side of the trench outline.

3 Remove blocks of sod from the trench outline, using a shovel. Cut sod 2" to 3" deep to keep roots intact. Place the sod on one of the plastic strips, and keep it moist.

4 Dig the trenches to the depth required by your local code. Heap the dirt onto the second strip of plastic.

(continued next page)

5 To run cable under a sidewalk, cut a length of metal conduit about 1 foot longer than width of sidewalk, then flatten one end of the conduit to form a sharp tip.

6 Drive the conduit through the soil under the sidewalk, using a ball-peen or masonry hammer and a wood block to prevent damage to the pipe. Cut off the ends of the conduit with a hacksaw, leaving about 2" of exposed conduit on each side. Underground cable will run through the conduit.

7 Attach a compression fitting and plastic bushing to each end of the conduit. The plastic fittings will prevent the sharp edges of the conduit from damaging the cable sheathing.

8 To tunnel under larger surfaces like driveways, make a water drill. Cut a piece of 1" steel pipe or intermediate metal conduit. Attach a threaded fitting for a garden hose on one end. Set the pipe in the trench, and use a scrap piece of lumber and a sledgehammer to drive the pipe as far under the driveway as possible. When the pipe won't go any farther, connect a garden hose to the end of the pipe and turn the water on. Continue pushing the pipe until the end emerges in the trench on the other side of the driveway.

3: Install Electrical Boxes & Conduit

How to Install Electrical Boxes & Conduit

Next, you'll attach the electrical boxes and the conduit through which the electrical cable will run. Use cast-aluminum or PVC boxes for outdoor fixtures, and install approved conduit to protect exposed cables. Don't use ordinary indoor boxes for outdoor applications; they're not watertight and are not legal for outdoor use. Some local codes require metal or plastic conduit to protect all underground cables, but in most regions this is not necessary. Many local codes allow you to use boxes and conduit made with PVC while others allow only cast-aluminum boxes and metal conduit.

Everything You Need:

NM two-wire cable, cable staples, plastic retrofit light fixture box with grounding clip, plastic single-gang retrofit boxes with internal clamps, extension ring, silicone caulk, IMC or rigid metal conduit, pipe straps, conduit sweep, compression fittings, plastic bushings, masonry anchors, single-gang outdoor boxes, galvanized screws, grounding pigtails, wire connectors.

How to Install Electrical Boxes & Conduit

1 Outline the GFCI receptacle box on the exterior wall. First drill pilot holes at the corners of the box outline, and use a piece of stiff wire to probe the wall for electrical wires or plumbing pipes. Complete the cutout with a jig saw or reciprocating saw. To make cutouts in masonry (inset), drill a line of holes inside the box outline, using a masonry bit, then remove waste material with a masonry chisel and ball-peen hammer.

2 From inside house, make the cutout for the indoor switch in the same stud cavity that contains the GFCI cutout. Outline the box on the wall, then drill a pilot hole and complete the cutout with a wallboard saw or jig saw.

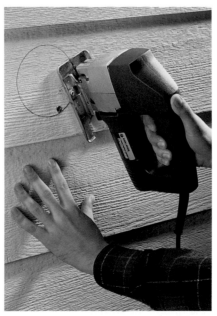

3 On outside of house, make the cutout for the motion-sensor light fixture in the same stud cavity with the GFCI cutout. Outline the light fixture box on the wall, then drill a pilot hole and complete the cutout with a wallboard saw or jig saw.

4 Estimate the distance between the indoor switch box and the outdoor motion-sensor box, and cut a length of NM cable about 2 feet longer than this distance. Use a fish tape to pull the cable from the switch box to the motion-sensor box.

(continued next page)

4: Install Underground Cable

Use UF (underground feeder) cable for outdoor wiring if the cable will come in direct contact with soil. UF cable has a solid-core vinyl sheathing and cannot be stripped with a cable ripper. Instead, use a utility knife and the method shown (steps 5 & 6, page opposite). Never use NM cable for outdoor wiring. If your local code requires that underground wires be protected by conduit, use THHN/THWN wire instead of UF cable.

After installing all cables, you are ready for the rough-in inspection. While waiting for the inspector, temporarily attach the weatherproof coverplates to the boxes or cover them with plastic to prevent moisture from entering. After the inspector has approved the rough-in work, fill in all cable trenches and replace the sod before making the final connections.

Everything You Need

UF cable, electrical tape, grounding pigtails, wire connectors, weatherproof coverplates.

How to Install Outdoor Cable

1 Measure and cut all cables, allowing an extra 12" at each box. At each end of the cable, use a utility knife to pare away about 3" of outer sheathing, leaving the inner wires exposed. Feed a fish tape down through the conduit from the GFCI box. Hook the wires at one end of the cable through the loop in the fish tape, then wrap electrical tape around the wires. Carefully pull the cable through the conduit.

2 Lay the cable along the bottom of the trench, making sure it is not twisted. Where cable runs under a sidewalk, use the fish tape to pull it through the conduit.

3 Use the fish tape to pull the end of the cable up through the conduit to the deck receptacle box at the opposite end of the trench. Remove the cable from the fish tape and cut away the bent end of the cable.

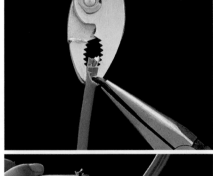
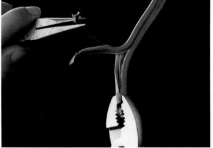

4 Bend back one of the wires, and grip it with needlenose pliers. Grip the cable with another pliers. Pull back on the wire, splitting the sheathing and exposing about 10" of wire. Repeat with the remaining wires, then cut off excess sheathing. Strip ¾" of insulation from the end of each wire.

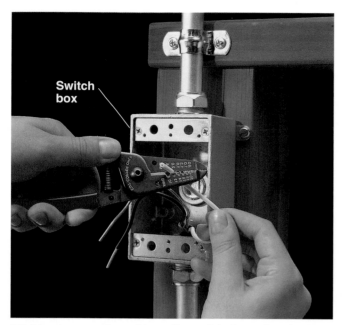

Switch box

5 Measure, cut, and install a cable from the deck receptacle box to the outdoor switch box, using the fish tape. Strip 10" of sheathing from each end of the cable, then strip ¾" of insulation from the end of each wire, using a combination tool.

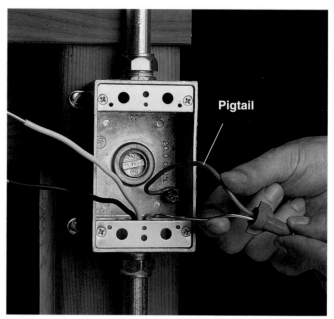

Pigtail

6 Attach a grounding pigtail to the back of each metal box and extension ring. Join all grounding wires with a wire connector. Tuck the wires inside the boxes, and temporarily attach the weatherproof coverplates until the inspector arrives for the rough-in inspection.

5: Make Final Connections

Make the final hookups for the switches, receptacles, and light fixtures after the rough-in cable installation has been reviewed and approved by your inspector, and after all trenches have been filled in. Install all the light fixtures, switches, and receptacles, then connect the circuit to the circuit breaker panel.

Because outdoor wiring poses a greater shock hazard than indoor wiring, the GFCI receptacle in this project is wired to provide shock protection for all fixtures controlled by the circuit.

When all work is completed and the outdoor circuit is connected at the service panel, your job is ready for final review by the inspector.

Everything You Need

Motion-sensor light fixture, GFCI receptacle, 15-amp grounded receptacle, outdoor switch, decorative light fixture, wire connectors.

How to Connect a Motion-sensor Light Fixture

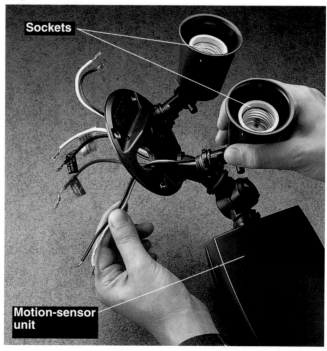

Sockets

Motion-sensor unit

1 Assemble fixture by threading the wire leads from the motion-sensor unit and the bulb sockets through the faceplate knockouts. Screw the motion-sensor unit and bulb sockets into the faceplate.

(continued next page)

Circuit Variation: Lamp Post

By slightly modifying the outdoor circuit installation (pages 50 to 61) you can add one or more permanent lamp posts to your landscape.

Digging trenches and running cables for this project is much the same, so the instructions here focus on the elements unique to the installation.

This, too, is a project calling for a good understanding of wiring principles. Make sure you're confident of your own abilities, and consider using professional help for areas where you're not well versed. For example, you might choose to dig the trenches and run the cables, but leave the final connections to an electrician.

How to Install a Lamp Post

Posts and lamps are are often sold separately. Posts are typically 7 ft. long and 3" in diameter and will fit any standard post lamp. Some include knockouts for photoelectric sensors and receptacles. Posts can be set directly in concrete or attached to a concrete pier using a base that is bolted to the pier (allowing easier replacement of damaged posts).

1 At each lamp post location, use a posthole digger to dig an 18"-deep hole for a concrete form tube. (Use a tube that is slightly wider than the lamp post's base). Cut tubes to length, so that about 2" will extend above the hole.

2 Mark the path for conduit from the post location to the GFCI outlet. Dig an 18"-deep trench along the path

3 Cut and join lengths of conduit with elbow fittings to hold the cables for each lamp post. If installing two posts, the first will have an inverted T fitting, while the other will be L-shaped. Position the conduit assemblies in the bottom of the holes, then cover them with a small amount of gravel. Lay UF cable in the trench and fish it up through the conduit (see page 58). Pour a small amount of gravel to cover the elbow fittings, then set the concrete forms in place over them.

4 While the concrete is still wet, place the J-bolts that will be used to mount the lamp post into the wet concrete. make sure to space them according to the lamp manufacturer's directions.

5 Place the post base on the J bolts and tighten the mounting nuts. Set the post in the base and secure it with the supplied screws.

6 Make the electrical connections for the lamp as directed by the manufacturer. Connect the black lead from the lamp to the black circuit wire with a wire connector. Connect the white lead from the lamp to the white circuit wire with a connector. Also connect the grounding wires together. Tuck the wires into the post, and secure the coverplate. Restore the power and test. Fill the trenches and replace the sod.

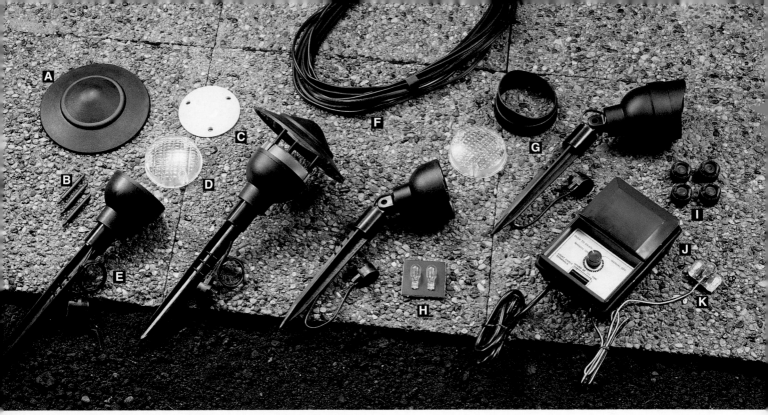

Typical low-voltage outdoor lighting system consists of: lens cap (A), lens cap posts (B), upper reflector (C), lens (D), base/stake/cable connector assembly (contains lower reflector) (E), low-voltage cable (F), lens hood (G), 7-watt 12-volt bulbs (H), cable connector caps (I), control box containing transformer and timer (J), light sensor (K).

Installing Low-voltage Lighting

Unlike some other outdoor wiring projects, low-voltage outdoor lighting systems don't require any expertise with electrical work. The basic system is simple: A transformer that you plug into any outlet carries 12-volt current through cables to individual fixtures. Installation is easy, and you don't need a permit or an inspection. Home improvement centers carry individual fixtures, transformers, and controls, as well as kits that bundle the components together in different configurations.

Transformers come in a wide range of sizes, from 40 watts to 900 watts, to fit lighting systems of different sizes. Individual light fixtures range from 15-watt accent lights for deck steps to 50-watt spotlights for highlighting a wall or tree.

To help plan, use a drawing of your landscape to mark the position of your lights. Purchase fixtures and the right transformers. Make a sketch of your yard, including locations of receptacles. Mark locations for lights, including decks, arbors, patios, and other features. Most designers recommend that pathways be lighted with a fixture every 8 to 10 ft.

After you've decided on the landscape features you want to light, you can plan the lighting style you want for each location (see photo above). A brochure from the lighting manufacturer can be very helpful here. Now, note the wattage of all the lights you plan to use and add them to your sketch. Add the wattages together and you'll get a sense of how big a transformer your system should have.

Make sure the transformer is rated for at least 25 watts more than the total wattage of the lights it will power. Oversizing the transformer will also give you options for expanding the system in the future. And try to avoid very long lighting loops, which cause a voltage drop that will make your lights dimmer than you want. For very large yards, it is best to install two or more lighting loops, each with its own transformer.

Everything You Need

Tools: Tape measure, drill, hammer, screwdriver, shovel, multimeter.

Materials: Low-voltage lighting kit, PVC conduit, conduit straps, caulk.

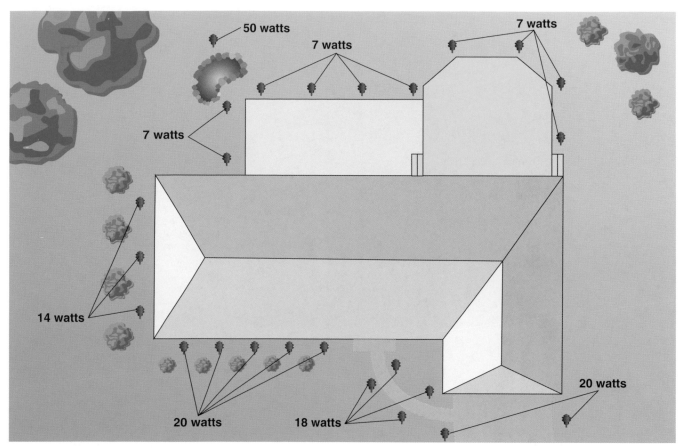

Make a diagram of your yard and mark the location of new fixtures. Note the wattages of the fixtures and use the diagram to select a transformer and plan the circuits.

Recommended cable lengths and gauges.

Circuit length	Cable gauge	Max watts
up to 100 ft.	16	150 W
100–150 ft.	14	200 W
150–200 ft.	12	300 W

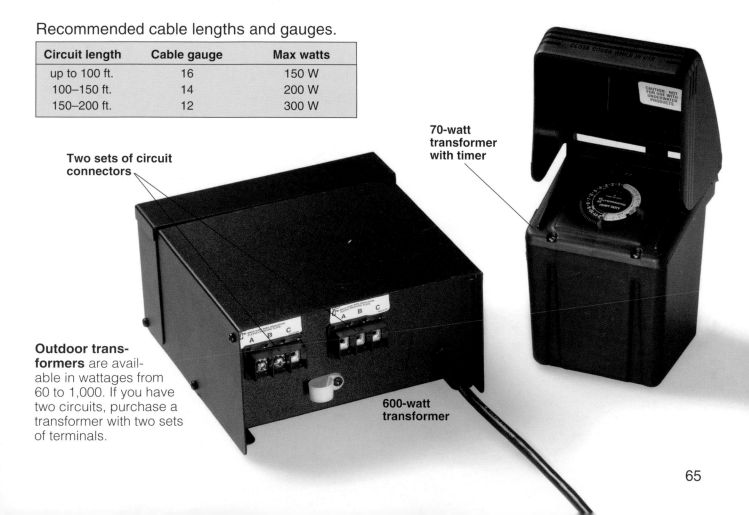

Two sets of circuit connectors

70-watt transformer with timer

Outdoor transformers are available in wattages from 60 to 1,000. If you have two circuits, purchase a transformer with two sets of terminals.

600-watt transformer

How to Install a Low-voltage Landscape Lighting Transformer

  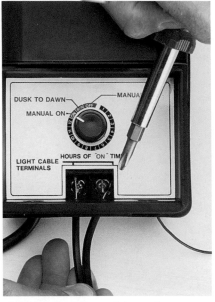

1 Install your transformer or transformers. If you are installing one in a garage, mount it on a wall within 24" of the GFCI receptacle and at least 12" off the floor. If you are using an outdoor receptacle on a wall or a post, mount the transformer on the same post or an adjacent post at least 12" off the ground and not more than 24" inches from the receptacle. Do not use an extension cord.

2 Drill a hole through the wall or rim joist for the low-voltage cable and any sensors to pass through (inset). If a circuit begins in a high-traffic area, it's a good idea to protect the cable by running it through a short piece of PVC pipe or conduit and then into the shallow trench.

3 Connect the cable to the transformer. Use the appropriate gauge cable for your circuit load (see page 51). Strip just enough insulation from the ends of the cable to make a good connection with the screw terminals. Make sure there is 10 ft. of cable between the transformer and the first fixture in the circuit. If you are running cable from a transformer on a post, staple the cable to the post an inch or two from the ground.

How to Install Low-voltage Landscape Light Circuits & Fixtures

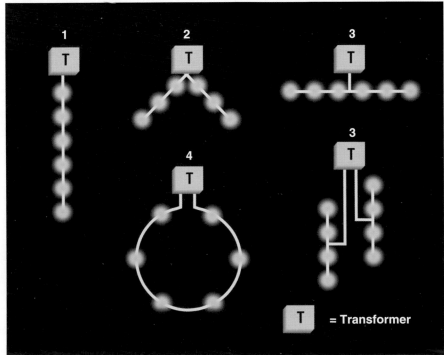

= Transformer

1 Select a circuit layout that avoids long runs of cable. This will minimize light-dimming voltage drop. Serial circuits (1) work best for simple designs with short cable runs. Split circuits (2) allow you to run two cables the maximum distance from the transformer. Tee circuits (3) distribute power evenly to lights that must be placed far from the transformer. You can also split the load over two tee circuits. For more compact designs, loop circuits (4) provide the most even power distribution. Use two transformers or a transformer with two sets of power outlets to create separate circuits that you can independently control (such as one circuit for path lights and another for landscape lights).

2 Lay the cables for each circuit. For routing around and under decks, use cable staples to hold the cable in place. Place the fixtures and connect their wires to the circuit cable. If drainpipes or irrigation systems are nearby, you may want to adjust the pipe or the fixture to minimize moisture contact. To create a branch circuit or to tie into an existing run, solder the wire connections or use plastic splice fittings (inset), which pierce insulation and provide a watertight connection. Use a multimeter to verify continuity on all splices.

3 Connect all the fixtures to the circuit cables. The fixture wires run from the fixture to the circuit cable and connect with special connectors that pierce the insulation on the cable and the wires to make a watertight connection. Most fixtures rest either in the ground or on a stake, but for fixtures mounted in trees, be sure any fasteners you use are stainless steel or cadmium-plated steel. Other materials may poison the tree.

4 Check to make sure the lights are working before you conceal the cable. You can use a multimeter to make sure you are getting 10 to 12 volts at the point where you want to install your fixture. (Losing two volts to voltage drop on any one circuit is considered acceptable.)

Variation: It's not necessary to bury most low-voltage cable in a trench (in fact, it's easier to diagnose problems if you leave the cable exposed or cover it with wood chips). In high-traffic areas like next to footpaths, sidewalks, or driveways, however, dig a shallow trench to protect cable runs. To run a cable under a sidewalk, use the technique shown on page 54. Test all cable runs with a multimeter for proper current (10–12 volts) before burying.

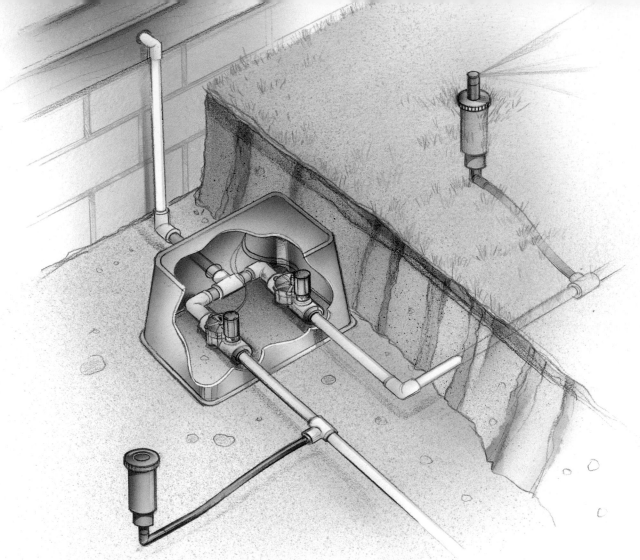

Installing an In-Ground Sprinkler System

Sprinkler systems offer a carefree means of keeping your lawn and garden green. Home improvement centers and landscaping retailers sell kits as well as individual components for installing in-ground systems. Installing a system can take a bit of time, but it's not at all difficult. The most challenging part of the job might be tapping into your home's plumbing system. If you're unsure of your abilities here, you can install everything but the final hookups, then hire a plumber to tap into the plumbing system.

For larger yards, design a sprinkler system with several zones, each serviced by a separate feeder pipe. Water is distributed to these zones at a manifold connected to the main supply line.

Before beginning an irrigation system project, check with your local building department. You may need a permit. Also check local requirements regarding backflow prevention or antisiphon devices. Before you dig trenches, call your utility company to have any utility lines marked.

A variety of timers are available for automating any irrigation system. More expensive models will control as many as 16 different zones, and may have rain sensors that prevent the system from operating if it is raining. The instructions will vary depending on the type of timer and accessory you buy, but all operate in largely the same way: the timer plugs into an ordinary receptacle, and sends its control signals to the manifold valves through low-voltage wires.

Everything You Need

Tools: Bucket, watch, pressure valve, drill with 1" bit, shovel, utility knife.

Materials: Compression T-fitting, PVC pipe, PVC valves & fittings, as needed, PVC solvent glue, antisiphon fitting (if required), irrigation manifold with control module & controller, wooden stakes & string, PVC or PE irrigation pipe, T-fittings & L-fittings, irrigation risers, irrigation heads.

How to Design an In-ground Sprinkler System

1 To measure the flow rate of your water service, set a gallon bucket under an outdoor spigot. Open the faucet all the way and record the amount of time it takes to fill the bucket. To calculate the gallons per minute (GPM), divide 60 by the number of seconds it took to fill the gallon bucket. So, if it took 6 seconds, the 60/6 equals 10 GPM. This number will determine the size of your manifold and feeder pipe.

2 Now measure the pressure of your water system. Make sure all faucets in the house are off. Attach a pressure valve to any faucet in the system and open its valve all the way. Record the reading.

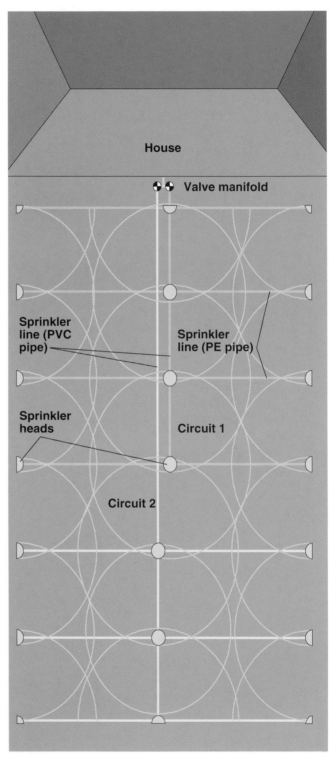

House

Valve manifold

Sprinkler line (PVC pipe)

Sprinkler line (PE pipe)

Sprinkler heads

Circuit 1

Circuit 2

3 Make a sketch showing layout of spinkler heads. Follow manufacturer's instructions for overlapping head spray patterns. Keep heads at least 6" from sidewalks, driveways, and buildings. Next, mark the irrigation manifold location and create zones for your sprinkler heads. Locate the manifold near the water meter. Zones are individual runs of PVC or PE supply pipe the same size as your water main. Turns and changes of elevation can reduce efficiency, so try to design zones with few turns or rises.

How to Install a Sprinkler System

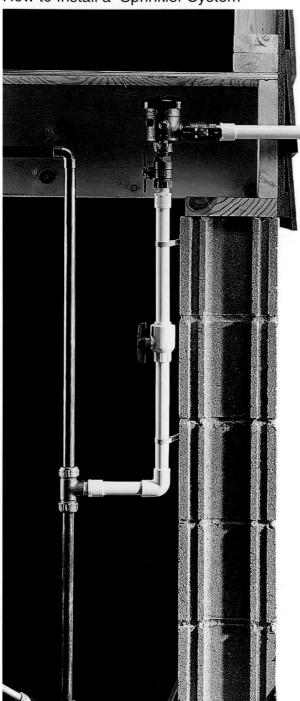

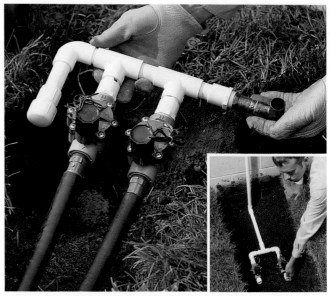

2 Choose a manifold with as many outlets as you have zones. The manifold shown here has two zones. Assemble the manifold as directed (some come preassembled, others are solvent-glued) and set it in the hole. Connect the supply pipe from the house to the manifold with an automated control module. install the controller on the house near the supply pipe (inset) and run the included wires under the supply pipe from the valves to control module.

1 Tap into your water supply. Shut off the water at the main shutoff valve. On the downstream side of your water meter, install a compression T-fitting. To supply the irrigation system, you will need to run PVC pipe to the manifold location. At a convenient location inside the house, install a gate valve with bleed in the line. Outside, dig a 10" trench leading to the manifold location. Drill a 1" hole through the sill directly above the trench, and route the pipe through the hole and down to the trench, using an L-fitting. You may also need to install a backflow prevention or an antisiphon device between the main and the irrigation manifold; check local code.

3 Mark the sprinkler locations. Use stakes or landscape flags to mark the sprinkler locations and then mark the pipe routes with spray paint or string. Once all the locations are marked, dig the trenches. In nonfreezing climates, trenches can be as little as 6". In freezing climates, dig trenches at least 10" deep. Renting a trencher can speed the job considerably. Set the sod aside so you can replace it after the sprinklers are installed.

4 Lay the pipe. Work on one zone at a time, beginning at the manifold. Connect the first section of PVC or PE pipe (PE shown) to the manifold outlet with solvent glue for PVC, or a barbed coupler and pipe clamps for PE (shown). At the first sprinkler location, connect a T-fitting with a female-threaded outlet for the riser. Continue with the next run of PE to the next sprinkler location. Install T-fittings at each sprinkler location. At the end of each zone, install an L-fitting for the last sprinkler.

5 Install the risers for the sprinkler heads. Risers come in a variety of styles. The simplest are short, threaded pipe nipples, but flexible and cut-to-fit risers are also available. Use a riser recommended by the manufacturer for your sprinkler head. For pop-up heads, make sure the nipple is the correct length for proper sprinkler operation.

6 Once all the risers are in place, flush the system. Turn on the water and open the valves for each zone one at a time, allowing the water to run for about a minute or until it runs clear. After the system is flushed, begin installing the sprinkler heads. Thread the heads onto the risers and secure them in place with earth. Make sure the heads are vertical (stake the risers if necessary). Fill in the rest of the trenches and replace the sod.

Variation: In freezing climates, it's a good idea to install a valve with a fitting that allows the system to be drained with compressed air. Install the fitting downstream of any antisiphon valves but before the manifold. In the fall, close the irrigation system's shutoff valve and open any drain valves. At the manifold, open one zone's valve and blow air into the zone until no water comes out. Repeat for each zone.

Installing a Drip Irrigation System

Installing a water-efficient drip irrigation system is very easy. A typical system consists of ½" plastic pipe that routes water from a hose spigot to trees, shrubs, and garden beds. The plastic tubing is fitted with small plastic nozzles, called emitters, at plant locations. Emitters are essentially mini-sprinklers, and they come in a variety of forms depending on the type of plant you need to water. If you're watering plant beds, assume you'll need 1 ft. of tubing with emitters for every square foot of plant bed space.

Everything You Need

Tools: Tubing punch.

Materials: Drip irrigation kit plus extra fittings, as needed.

Drip irrigation systems offer many different types of fittings, including the spray head shown here. Because they precisely direct water exactly where it's needed, drip systems waste very little water. A thick layer of mulch around plants will also help keep soil moist.

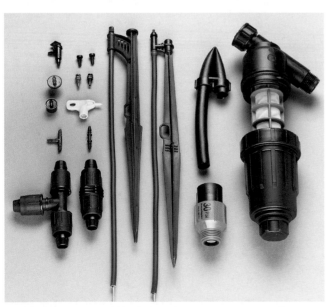

Basic kits come with only a few components, but can be augmented with pieces purchased "ala carte." You'll also need a punch for piercing the tubing and "goof plugs" for repairing errant punches.

Tubing for drip irrigation is thin-wall flexible polyethylene or polyvinyl, typically ¼" or ½" in diameter. Internal diameters can vary from manufacturer to manufacturer, so it's a good idea to purchase pipe and fittings from a single source.

How to Install a Drip Irrigation System

1 Connect the system's supply tube to a water source, such as a hose spigot or a rain water system. If you tap into your household water supply, use a pressure gauge to check water pressure (page 69). If pressure exceeds 50 pounds per square inch (psi), install a pressure-reducing fitting before attaching the feeder tube. A filter should also be attached to the faucet before the feeder tube.

2 At garden bed locations, begin installing drip emitters every 18". You can also purchase ½" PE tubing with emitters preinstalled. If you use this tubing, cut the feeder tub once it reaches the first bed, and attach the emitter tubing with a barbed coupling. Route the tubing among the plants so that emitters are over the roots.

3 For trees and shrubs, make a branch loop around the tree. Pierce the feed tube near the tree and insert a T-fitting. Loop the branch around the tree and connect it to both outlets on the T-fitting. Use ¼" tubing for small trees, ½" for larger specimens. Insert emitters in the loop every 18".

4 Use micro sprayers for hard-to-reach plants. Sprayers can be connected directly to the main feeder line or positioned on short branch lines. Sprayers come in a variety of spray patterns and flow rates; chose one most appropriate for the plants to be watered.

5 Potted plants and raised beds can also be watered with sprayers. Place stake-mounted sprayers in the pots or beds. Connect a length of ¼" tubing to the feeder line with a couple, and connect the ¼" line to the sprayer.

6 Once all branch lines and emitters are installed, flush the system by turning on the water and let it flow for a full minute. Then, close the ends of the feeder line and the branch lines with figure-8 end crimps. Tubing can be left exposed or buried under mulch.

Installing a Rain Barrel Irrigation System

One of the simplest, least expensive ways to irrigate a landscape is with a system that collects and stores rainwater for controlled distribution either through a garden hose or a drip irrigation system.

The most common system includes one or more rain barrels (typically 40 to 80 gallons in capacity) connected to downspouts. Valve fittings at the bottoms of the barrels let you connect them to a hose or to a drip irrigation line. The system can be configured as a primary irrigation system or a secondary system to augment a standard irrigation system.

Some communities now offer subsidies for rain barrel use, offering free or reduced-price barrels and downspout connection kits. Check with your local water authorities.

Everything You Need

Tools: Drill, hacksaw.

Materials: Rain barrel kit, downspout diverter (optional), pavers or blocks (optional).

How to Install a Rain Barrel System

1 Select a location for the barrel under a downspout. Locate your barrel as close to the area you want to irrigate as possible. Make sure the barrel has a stable, level base. Connect the overflow tube, and make sure it is pointed away from the foundation.

2 Connect the spigot near the bottom of the barrel. Some kits may include a second spigot for filling watering cans. Use Teflon tape at all threaded fittings to ensure a tight seal. Remove the downspout, and set the barrel on its base.

3 Cut the downspout to length with a hacksaw. Reconnect the elbow fitting to the downspout, using sheetmetal screws. Attach the cover to the top of the rain barrel. Some systems include a cover with porous wire mesh, to which the downspout delivers water. Others include a cover with a sealed connection (next step).

4 Link the downspout elbow to the rain barrel with a length of flexible downspout extension attached to the elbow and the barrel cover.

Variation: If your barrel comes with a downspout adapter, cut away a segment of downspout and insert the adapter so it diverts water into the barrel.

5 Connect a drip irrigation tube or garden hose to the spigot. A Y-fitting, like the one shown here, will let you feed the drip irrigation system through a garden hose when the rain barrel is empty.

6 If you want, increase water storage by connecting two or more rain barrels together with a linking kit, available from many kit suppliers.

Installing a Garden Spigot

You may already have a hose spigot or two attached to the foundation of your house, but adding one or two spigots to various areas of your outdoor home brings water right to the areas where you typically water plants or clean up garden equipment.

To install a garden spigot, run a branch line off your home's water supply system, through the foundation or exterior wall, and along an underground trench to a hose spigot anchored to a post, which is embedded in a bucket of concrete at the end of the plumbing run.

The project illustrated here uses copper pipe for the aboveground parts of the run, and PE pipe for the buried sections. Your local plumbing code may have requirements for the types of pipe you can use, so check it before you begin. Also, if local plumbing code requires it, be sure to apply for required permits and arrange for necessary inspections.

Everything You Need

Tools: Spade, drill, tubing cutters, soldering materials, screwdrivers.

Materials: Copper T-fittings, ¾" copper pipe, gate valve with bleed, copper elbows, vacuum breaker, stakes, valve boxes (2), ¾" PE pipe, PVC couplings, stainless steel clamps, 4-ft. 4 × 4 post, spigot, pipe straps, concrete, 2-gallon plastic bucket, barbed PVC T-fittings with threaded outlet and plug (2), male-threaded copper adapters (2), female-threaded PE adapters (2).

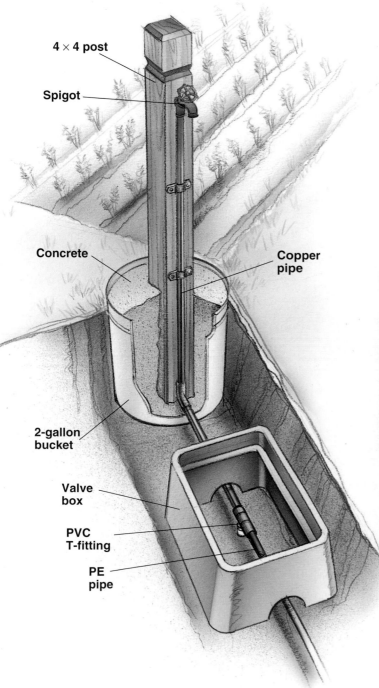

4 × 4 post

Spigot

Concrete

Copper pipe

2-gallon bucket

Valve box

PVC T-fitting

PE pipe

How to Install a Garden Spigot

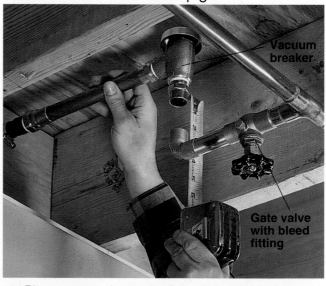

Vacuum breaker

Gate valve with bleed fitting

1 Plan a convenient route from the water supply line in the house to the spigot location. Drill a 1" hole through the exterior wall. Turn off the water at the main supply valve. Remove a small section of cold water pipe and install a T-fitting. Install a straight length of copper pipe, then a gate valve with a bleed fitting. Use straight pipes and elbows to extend the branch line through the hole in the wall, installing a vacuum breaker at some point along the way.

2 Outside the house, stake a line marking the path for the pipe run to the spigot location. Use a trenching spade to remove sod for an 8"- to 12"-wide trench along the marked route. Dig a trench at least 10" deep and sloping toward the house at a rate of ⅛" per foot. Dig a hole for a valve box, directly below the point where the branch line exits the house. Measure, cut, and attach copper pipe and elbows, extending the branch line down to the bottom of the trench and out 12". Install a valve box with the top flush to the ground.

3 Dig a hole at the spigot location to hold a valve box and bucket. Create an L-shaped spigot assembly using a 3-ft. copper pipe, a copper elbow, a 2-ft. copper pipe, and a hose spigot. Solder the pieces together. Cut a 1" hole in the side of the plastic bucket, then thread the copper assembly through the bottom of the hole. Position the bucket and valve box in the ground. Insert the wooden post into the bucket and secure the copper assembly to it with pipe straps. Fill the bucket with concrete, using a level to make sure the post is plumb.

Spigot valve box.
Shown cutaway.

T-fitting
with plug

4 Lay ¾" PE pipe in the trench, running from the valve box by the house to the valve box at the spigot location. Use couplings and stainless steel clamps when necessary to join two lengths of pipe.

5 At both valve boxes, install a T-fitting with a threaded outlet, facing down, onto the PE pipe inside the valve box. Cap the outlet with a plug. At the spigot box, use threaded adapters to join the copper pipe to the PE pipe. Restore the water and test the line for leaks. Replace the sod.

6 To drain the pipe for the winter, close the valve for the outdoor supply pipe, then remove the cap on the drain nipple. With the faucet on the outdoor spigot open, attach an air compressor to the drain nipple, then blow water from the system, using no more than 50 psi of pressure. Remove the plugs from the Ts in the valve boxes and store them for the winter.

Installing an Outdoor Sink

If you're a backyard cook or a gardener, an outdoor sink is a convenient addition to your patio or potting shed.

Building an outdoor sink can be as easy as making a cutout for a stainless-steel self-rimming sink in a potting bench. Other options include building a sink base out of concrete block or bricks. You can also purchase outdoor kitchen cabinets and mount the sink in countertop made from weather-resistant material.

Unless you plan to wash dishes and send a lot of organic matter down the sink, it probably won't be necessary to connect the sink to your home's plumbing drain system. Running a drain line from the sink to a dry well is sufficient for most needs. Check local code for specific requirements.

Everything You Need

Tools: Spade, pipe wrench, jigsaw, drill.

Materials: Sink cabinet and countertop or potting bench, stainless-steel self-rimming sink, drain and P-trap assemblies, faucet and supply hose, landscape fabric, gravel, 1½" PVC pipe and fittings, solvent glue and primer.

How to Install an Outdoor Sink

1 Position the bench or base cabinet. Make sure it's in a location that gives you a clear path to an existing dry well or is near a place where you can dig a new one. Trace the outline of the sink onto the countertop, and make the cutout, using a jigsaw.

2 Dig a trench from the patio edge to a dry well (page 38). Dig the trench at least 10" deep, sloping toward the dry well. Line the trench with landscape fabric and a 1" layer of gravel. From the dry well, run 1½" perforated PVC pipe to the patio location.

3 With the sink upside down on a workbench, install the drain and trap fittings on the sink. Lay a bead of silicone caulk around the edge of the sink cutout in the bench and set the sink in the cutout. If the sink is secured with clips, tighten the clips.

4 Use PVC pipes and elbow fittings joined with solvent glue to connect the drain tailpiece to the perforated pipe leading to the dry well. Cover the trench and replace the sod.

5 Install the faucet in the sink cutouts. In most cases, a cold-water line will be sufficient. Connect a garden hose from a nearby hose bib to the faucet supply pipe.

6 For permanent installations, route copper supply pipes from a nearby indoor supply line through the exterior wall and into the cabinet. Install shutoff valves and connect to the faucet with flexible supply tubes.

Installing an Outdoor Shower

Outdoor showers have become popular amenities for modern landscapes. For pool and hot tub owners and for oceanside homes, they're a convenient place to wash off chlorine and salt.

Retailers sell a variety of outdoor shower kits. Some require dedicated hot and cold lines, but most simply connect to a garden hose. Few showers have any provision for drainage, which can present a runoff problem. The project that follows shows you how to build an attractive shower surround over a dry well (see page 38). Depending on your yard and how you plan to use the shower, you may want to build a full or partial enclosure for the shower. The steps below show a complete enclosure.

Everything You Need

Tools: Spade, power auger or posthole digger, stakes, string, wheelbarrow.

Materials: Plastic trash can, landscape fabric, large stones to fill trash can, concrete, 4 10-ft. pressure-treated, cedar, or redwood 4 x 4s, 3 4 x 8 cedar, or redwood lattice privacy panels, 3 10-ft. pressure-treated, cedar, or redwood 2 x 4s, 12 10-ft. pressure-treated, cedar, or redwood 1 x 4s, 12 pressure-treated, cedar, or redwood 1 x 1s, 10d galvanized nails, 6d galvanized nails, construction adhesive.

How to Build an Outooor Shower

1 At the shower location, outline the shower base on the ground, and create a dry well (page 38). The dry well is simply a plastic garbage container punched with holes and filled with gravel or crushed stone. The top of the garbage can should sit level with the surrounding sod. Backfill soil around the dry well.

2 Dig holes and install posts for the surround. Our example has walls on two sides, so we've set three posts to create an L-shaped surround with 4-ft. wide walls, 77" tall. Locate the surround so that there are at least 12" between the edges of the shower deck and the walls. Brace the posts so they are plumb, then fill the holes with concrete. Smooth the tops of the post footings with a trowel.

3 Build walls for the shower surround. We've used PVC lattice pannels cut to size, but other materials can also be used. Secure the wall panels to the posts with corrosion-resistant screws.

4 Once the surround is complete, place the outdoor shower unit inside the enclosure, positioning it so that it is entirely over the dry well. Connect the shower to a nearby hose bib.

Lawns & Gardens

Even if you're not a gardener, a good portion of your landscape involves living plants in some fashion. Building landscape walls, for example, may mean installing a hedge. Your landscape's floor may be grass sod, not a brick paver patio. This section will both show you the process of installing the basic plantings of your landscape, and also give directions for a variety of structures used to hold ornamental plantings, such as rock gardens and raised garden beds made from landscape timbers.

• **Improving your soil** (page 84).

• **Installing & repairing lawns** (page 86).

• **Installing lawn edging** (page 92).

• **Creating planting beds** (page 94).

• **Building a raised garden** (page 96).

• **Building a rock garden** (page 98).

• **Planting trees & shrubs** (page 100).

• **Removing trees** (page 102).

• **Planting hedges** (page 104).
• **Pruning trees & shrubs** (page 105).

Leaves

Grass

Peat moss

Compost

Straw

Manure

Organic amendments are the best choice for improving the structure and nutrient levels of your soil.

Improving Your Soil

In addition to creating the foundation for your entire landscape, your soil provides the water and nutrients your plants, lawn, trees, and shrubs need to develop large, healthy root systems. Very few yards, however, are blessed with perfect soil that provides an ideal growing environment. You'll probably need to amend your soil to improve its structure and nutrient levels. Whenever possible, amend the soil early in the landscaping process, when the task is easier and yields better results.

Requesting a Soil Test

To get the most accurate assessment of how to improve your soil, have it analyzed by a soil testing lab. For a small fee, a local lab or your state's agricultural extension service will conduct a detailed analysis of a soil sample from your yard.

In general, it takes anywhere from three to six weeks to receive the results of a soil analysis, so send the samples long before you plan to begin landscaping. Include written information with the sample, detailing what you've added to your soil in the past—such as fertilizers, lime, peat moss or compost. Also, include information on the specific plants you want to grow. The lab will provide a report that suggests specific amendments to add to your soil to support the plants you'll be growing.

How to collect a soil sample

1 For each area where you intend to plant, dig a 1-ft.-deep hole, using a clean shovel. Cut a ½"-wide slice from the top to the bottom of the hole, using the shovel. Remove the top ½" off of the slice, and place the remaining portion in a clean bucket. Repeat this process in at least five different areas of the planting site, mixing each of the slices together in the bucket.

2 Pour about one pint of the sample soil into a clean container, such as a locking plastic bag. Mail the sample and the written information to the soil testing lab.

How to Read a Soil Test Report

Nitrogen is necessary for developing healthy leaf and stem growth.

Phosphorus is needed for strong, healthy root systems.

Soil texture is classified as one of eleven soil types.

Soil pH measures the acidity or alkalinity of your soil sample.

Potassium promotes flower growth in annuals and perennials.

Recommendations for lawn growth tell you how to improve your soil to support a lawn.

Recommendations for vegetable and flower gardens specify how to amend the soil to foster successful gardens.

Soil Test Report

Sample No.
008

Soil Texture
Sandy Loam

Soil pH
6.8

Nitrogen (N) (ppm)
20

Phosphorus (P) (ppm)
15

Potassium (K) (ppm)
125

	Very Low	Low	Medium	High	Very High
Nitrogen (N)					
Phosphorus (P)					
Potassium (K)					

Soil PH

3 Acid 4 5 6 7 Optimum 8 9 Alkaline

Recommendations for Home Lawn: The approximate ratio or proportion of these nutrients is: 5-0-5. Apply according to the instructions on the fertilizer bag or container. Since meeting the exact amount required for each nutrient will not be possible in most cases, it is more important to apply the amount of nitrogen required and compromise some for phosphate and potash. Grass clippings left on the lawn is a sound practice.

For Vegetable and Flower Gardens: Manure, compost, or other forms of organic matter may be added. These amendments provide a good source of trace nutrients and improve soil granulation. Three to five bushels of manure or compost per 100 sq. ft. are recommended.

The soil test report details your soil's texture and it's pH and nutrient levels. It will also tell you how to improve the soil in order to grow the plants you want.

Texture. Soil texture is categorized as loamy, sandy, silty, clayey or a combination of two of these categories, such as loamy-sand or silty-clay. Loamy soil is ideal for growing plants—it is composed of almost equal amounts of sand, silt, and clay. Because sandy soil doesn't retain water or nutrients, plants must be frequently watered and fertilized. Silty soil holds moisture and nutrients fairly well. However, it cannot absorb a lot of water at once and requires frequent, light waterings. Clayey soil holds moisture and nutrients well, but is too dense for root growth and too damp for plants that require well-drained soil.

The soil test report will suggest organic amendments, such as compost, manure, or peat moss, to improve sandy, silty, and clayey soils. In sandy and silty soils,

organic material helps retain moisture for plant roots. In clayey soils, amendments help loosen the soil, improving breathability and drainage.

Soil pH is a value of the soil's acidity or alkalinity based on a scale from 0 to 14. The report will identify your soil's pH, and tell you the ideal pH for growing the plants you specified. If your soil is very acidic or alkaline, you may need to alter your plant selection. Fertility is a measure of the quantity of nitrogen, phosphorus, and potassium in the soil. The report will measure the presence of each element in parts per million (ppm), and rate each measurement as low, medium, or high.

Specific recommendations. Amending poor soils with organic materials boosts nutrient levels and improves the soil's structure. The results of your soil test will suggest how you can amend your soil to foster lawn and plant growth.

Installing & Repairing Lawns

Preparing the Soil

Soil preparation is the most important step in establishing new lawns and planting areas. Start by testing the soil (page 85). The test will tell you the type of soil, the nutrient levels present, and whether it is capable of supporting a lawn. The report will also include detailed instructions for amending and fertilizing the lawn. If your soil fails the lawn compatibility test, don't despair. You can purchase high-quality topsoil to add to your existing soil. Topsoil, also called "black dirt," is sold by the cubic yard and can be delivered by soil contractors.

Starting the Lawn

From there, you have two options for starting a new lawn: seed or sod. Seed is the easiest and least expensive way to start a lawn. The best time to seed is during the growing season for grass shoots. The timing of this will depend on where you live. In warmer climates, shoot growth primarily occurs in the spring. In cooler climates, there are two growth seasons—one in the early spring and another in the early fall. Many experts feel that fall is the ideal time to seed lawns in colder climates because fewer weeds are present and frequent rains and cool temperatures keep the grass seed moist.

Your second option, installing sod, is the quicker way to a new lawn. Within hours, you can transform bare dirt into a lush lawn. Sod can be installed at any time from the beginning of the spring through early fall, but avoid installing it during especially hot, dry weather. Purchase sod from a sod farm, landscape supply store, or landscape contractor. For the best results, ask that sod be delivered within 24 hours of being cut. After the sod arrives, store it in a shaded area, and lay it within a day, keeping it moist but not soggy.

Once the sod is laid, keep it constantly moist for three days. Water regularly thereafter.

Repairing a Lawn

Established lawns may eventually need renovation. The process involves diagnosing and repairing lawn problems; then topseeding and fertilizing the lawn to grow new, healthy grass. Typical conditions corrected during renovation include an abundance of weeds, large bare areas, excessive thatch, and soil compaction.

Start out by testing your soil. Then, determine what weeds currently are present in your lawn, and evaluate the balance between weeds and grass. If over 40 percent of your lawn consists of weeds, simple renovation won't solve the problem—experts recommend demolishing the lawn and starting over again from scratch.

Cut a small, 6"-deep, pie-shaped wedge out of your lawn as a sample. This will let you measure the level of thatch, the layer of partially decomposed pieces of grass sitting on top of the soil. Healthy lawns include a moderate layer of thatch, but if the thatch is more than ½" thick, add thatch removal to your renovation plan. Also, check the moisture content of the soil in the wedge. If the soil isn't moist all the way to the bottom, you need to add water. The soil should be moist to a depth of 6" before you begin work, which could take days to achieve.

Everything You Need

Tools: Tiller, rake, level, stakes, mason's string, landscape drum, broadcast spreader, sod knife, pressure sprayer, vertical mower, leaf rake, aerator,goggles, particle mask, soil test report.

Materials: Recommended amendment, topsoil, grass seed or sod, flour, weed killer, fertilizer, grass seed.

How to Prepare the Soil

1 If the test report indicates that you need to amend the soil, purchase the recommended amendments and rent a tiller to blend them into the soil. Set the tiller to a depth of 4" to 6". Spread an even layer of the amendments over the surface of a small area and till them into the soil. Work your way across the yard in the same pattern you would use for mowing. Once the entire area is tilled, regrade and level the soil as necessary.

2 Prepare the existing soil to mix with the new topsoil by loosening it with a tiller or, if it's heavily compacted, hiring a contractor to "slice" it with heavy machinery outfitted with a blade. Order enough topsoil to spread a 4" layer over the entire area. The contractor can also distribute the soil. To do it yourself, drop wheelbarrow loads of soil around the area, then use a rake to distribute the soil evenly. Check and correct the grade of the yard (page 34).

3 To create a smooth, even surface for seeding, sodding, or planting ground cover, you'll need to slightly compress the soil. The goal is to smooth the surface without compacting the soil. Fill a landscape drum ⅓ full with water, then roll it over the surface, walking in a row-by-row pattern.

Tip: Grass seed or sod— what choice is best for you?

If you're starting a new lawn, you'll want to choose the method that works best for your situation. Seeding and sodding each have benefits, as well as drawbacks. Time, money, climate, maintenance requirements and the amount of stress the lawn will endure are all factors to take into account as you choose the best method for establishing a new lawn.

Sod
- Expensive
- Immediate results
- Limited variety of grasses
- Establishes well on slopes
- Fewer weeds
- Heavy work

Seed
- Inexpensive
- Takes longer to develop
- Wide variety of grasses
- Establishes strong root systems
- Ideal planting times limited
- Daily watering

How to Seed a New Lawn

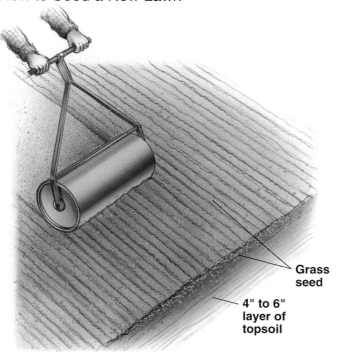

The goal is to spread seed over a 4" to 6" layer of topsoil and then to lightly compact the soil and the seed.

1 Prepare the soil as shown on page 87. Water the soil until it's moist to a depth of 4" to 6". Place a broadcast spreader on a paved surface, such as a driveway. Fill the spreader with the amount of grass recommended on the seed package.

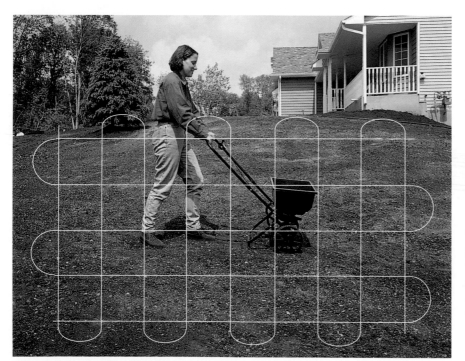

2 Establish the desired rate of seed coverage by calibrating the spreader according to the recommendations on the seed package. Apply the seed in two stages, following a grid pattern to ensure even coverage. First, push the spreader back and forth across the yard in straight passes. When you've covered the entire area, push the spreader up and down the yard, perpendicular to the first application. Lightly rake the soil until only 10–15 percent of the seed is visible.

3 Lightly compact the raked soil by rolling over it with a half-filled landscape drum. Water the yard until the soil is moist to a depth of 6", then keep the seed moist for several weeks.

How to Install a Sod Lawn

1 Prepare the soil. Select a straight border, such as a walkway, to use as a reference guide. If there isn't a straight surface in the immediate area, sprinkle flour on the ground as a reference line. Working parallel to your reference guide, install the first roll of sod. Firmly push the sod into the soil. Continue placing rolls parallel to the guide, butting the seams as close together as possible. To help eliminate the appearance of seams, stagger the ends of the rolls.

2 Lift the edges of pieces that butt against each other, then press the edges down, knitting the two pieces together. As each new piece is laid, cover the seams with ½" of topsoil to prevent the edges from drying out.

3 Continue laying the sod, staggering the end seams. When sodding a slope, drive wooden stakes through the sod, 4" to 6" into the soil, to hold the sod in place. Use a sod knife to trim excess sod around walkway curves, planting beds, and trees.

4 Roll over the sod with a half-filled landscape drum, pressing the sod firmly into the soil. Water the sod until it's thoroughly saturated.

How to Renovate a Lawn

1 Spot-kill the weeds in your lawn by applying weed killer, using a pressure sprayer. Wear gloves, safety goggles, a particle mask, and protective clothing when using weed killer. Use a broadleaf herbicide to kill broadleaf weeds, such as dandelion and clover. For grassy weeds, such as crabgrass and quackgrass, use a nonselective herbicide containing glyphosate. Glyphosate kills all grass, plants, shrubs or trees it comes into contact with, so apply it carefully, and plan to replant affected areas.

2 Remove thatch with a rented vertical mower, also called a power rake. Set the tines on the vertical mower to rake about ¼" below the surface of the soil. Push the vertical mower over the entire lawn in a series of straight passes, then go over it again in perpendicular rows, covering the area in a grid pattern. Rake up and discard the removed thatch

3 Relieve soil compaction and improve drainage by removing small cores of soil from your lawn with a rented aerator. Run the machine across the lawn, using the same grid pattern described in Step 2. Let the soil cores partially dry, then rake them up. Using the vertical mower or a leaf rake, scratch the entire surface of the lawn to loosen the soil slightly.

4 Fill a broadcast spreader with the fertilizer blend recommended in the soil test report. Calibrate the spreader according to the directions on the fertilizer package. Distribute the fertilizer, covering the lawn in perpendicular rows. Fill the spreader with grass seed. Topseed the entire lawn.

Lawn Renovation Tips

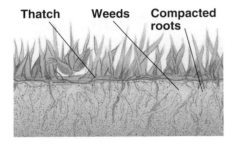

Thatch   Weeds   Compacted roots

Aerated soil   Grass seed

A lawn choked with weeds and excess thatch (top) will be more prone to bare spots and brown patches. Weed abatement, thatch removal, aeration, and reseeding create the proper conditions for healthy lawn growth (below).

Tip: Repairing Bare Spots

If your lawn is plagued with dying areas, you'll need to determine the cause and take preventive measures to keep the grass from dying again. Once the problem is solved, sprinkle grass seed over the bare area, lightly rake it into the soil, and gently tamp the soil down. Keep the area moist for at least two weeks while the seed germinates. Use the following guidelines to resolve common problems:

Cause	Solution
Dog damage	Immediately water areas where the dog urinates.
Compacted soil	Aerate the area, or till in an amendment, such as compost or peat moss.
Chemical burn	Remove several inches of topsoil from the bare area.
Disease	Consult your local extension service for diagnosis and treatment.
Foot traffic	Install a path or stepping stones to accommodate traffic.
Insects	Consult your local extension service for recommendations.

Tip: Reading Grass Seed Labels

The type of grass you select will play a large part in the success of your lawn. But it can be difficult to tell exactly what you're buying. Whether it's a prepackaged blend or seed sold by the pound in bulk, there will always be a label that tells you exactly what type of seeds are included in that blend.

Lush Lawn Blend, Grass Seed & Supply Co., Fairtown, MN Lot. No.: 5546-89, Test Date: 06/06/98

Pure Seed	Variety	Germination
42%	Colonel Kentucky Bluegrass	88%
33%	Fine Perennial Ryegrass	78%
21%	Red Tall Fescue	80%
0.4%	Inert Matter	
1.2%	Crop	
2.4%	Weed	

Pure Seed: the percentage of seeds for each variety that are capable of growing.

Germination: the portion of the pure seed that will germinate within a reasonable amount of time.

Inert Matter: materials present in the blend, such as broken seeds, hulls, and chaff, that aren't capable of growing.

Crop: the percentage of agricultural grain and undesirable grass seed contained in the blend.

Weed: the portion of weed seeds present in the blend.

Installing Lawn Edging

Lawn edging is no more than a divider between grass and another area, like a planting bed or a walkway, but it can make your landscape a lot more attractive and a lot easier to care for. Installing edging helps contain mulch materials in planting areas and keep lawn grass from encroaching on garden beds.

Many different materials can be used for edgings, some of which are shown below. On the facing page, you'll learn a method for installing an elegant brick edging.

Everything You Need

Tools: Spade, rubber mallet, hand trowel.

Materials: Bricks, sand, landscape fabric.

Many materials that can be used for edgings are shown here. From top: landscape timbers, flagstone, cast concrete pavers, clay brick, synthetic stone blocks, natural stone, and plastic edging.

Plastic edging is one of the most inexpensive options. To install, you simply cut a narrow trench with a spade, insert the edging, and secure it with spikes.

How-to Install Brick Lawn Edging

1 Lay out your gaden site and prepare the soil, then test-fit the brick edging. Gaps should be no more than ½" wide. When satisfied with the layout, outline the edging with string and remove the bricks.

2 Dig out the edging area to create a flat-bottomed trench about ½" deeper than the depth at which you plan to lay the bricks. For example, for 1½" thick bricks laid at ground level, dig a 3" deep trench.

3 Place a ½" deep layer of sand in the edging tench, and level it with the blade of a spade. The sand provides a firm, stable base for the brick edging.

4 Lay a strip of landscape fabric in the trench over the layer of sand; then lay the bricks side by side in the trench. The landscape fabric helps prevent weeds from growing up through the soil and sand.

5 Set the bricks by laying a 2 × 4 on edge over them and tapping it with a with a rubber mallet. Adjust uneven bricks by tapping them directly with the mallet or by lifting the bricks and adding more sand.

6 Spread sand over the bricks and gently work it into the cracks with a broom. Packing sand in the cracks helps to inhibit weeds and stabilizes the bricks. From time to time, it may be necessary to add more sand.

Creating Planting Beds

Planting beds provide a natural finishing touch to a yard—a place to grow ornamental flowers and shrubs or even a vegetable garden.

Professional landscapers tell us that the most common mistake among amateur landscapers is to devote far too little space to planting areas. Many designers suggest that planting areas should occupy 40 to 50 percent of the total open yard area. In addition to offering ornament, creating spacious planting areas can save you time on lawn care. When properly installed and mulched, a planting bed doesn't need much maintenance.

But the soil in your planting area may need to be improved in order to grow healthy flowers and shrubs in your planting area. A soil test (page 85) is a good idea before you begin. A variety of soil amendments are available to make your soil more friendly to ornamental plants.

Everything You Need

Tools: Hose, spade, shovel.

Materials: Plastic edging, landscape fabric (optional), soil builders, mulch, plants.

Organic soil builders, including composted manure, peat moss, and bone meal, improve soil in the same way as chemical additives but pose less danger to the environment from rainwater runoff.

How to Install a Planting Bed

1 Use a garden hose to outline the planned garden bed area. Remove the ground cover inside the area with a spade.

2 Dig a trench around the perimeter of the bed using a spade. Place plastic lawn edging in the trench and secure it by driving edging stakes through the bottom lip.

3 Till amendments into the soil with a spade and shovel. Test the design and layout of the plants. Install landscaping fabric over the entire area if desired to inhibit weed growth.

4 Plant the plants in the bed. Apply a 2" to 3" layer of mulch over the entire surface.

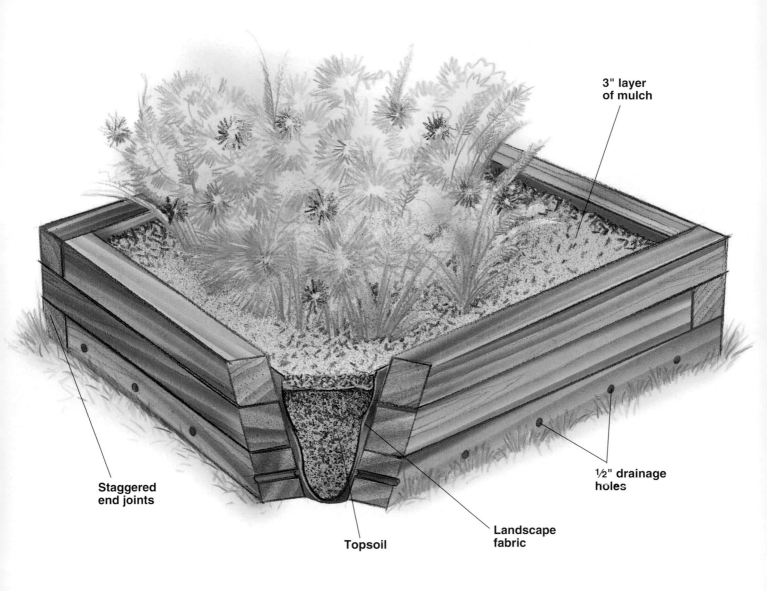

3" layer of mulch

Staggered end joints

Topsoil

Landscape fabric

½" drainage holes

Building a Raised Garden

Raised garden beds are attractive, functional, and easy to maintain. Because these gardens are elevated, they are perfect for children as well as physically disabled or older family members. They provide excellent opportunities to repeat materials used in other landscape elements, while creating visually appealing design. Keep in mind that any plants placed in a raised garden bed will require additional watering due to the raise in grade.

Raised planting beds can be built from a variety of building materials. This raised planting bed uses 4 × 4 cedar posts stacked on top of each other in three layers. Composite timber material (page 10) or pressure-treated lumber are other material options using the same construction methods. Apply a coat of wood sealer/protectant to the cut timbers and allow it to dry completely before placing them in the ground

Everything You Need

Tools: Basic tools (page18), reciprocating saw, drill with bits, stakes and string.

Materials: 8-ft. 4 × 4 timbers (6), 6" galvanized nails, landscape fabric, galvanized roofing nails, topsoil, plantings, mulch, wood sealer/protectant.

How to Build a Raised Garden

Tip: Planting & Maintaining a Raised Garden Bed

Raised-bed gardens freeze faster and deeper than in-ground planting beds. Because the outside edges of the bed are more sensitive to temperature fluctuations, use this space for annuals and hardy perennials. Plant sensitive perennials and bulbs closer to the center, where the soil temperature is more stable.

If you live in an area with below-freezing winter temperatures, limit your plant choices to winter-hardy perennials, annual flowers, and vegetables.

Raised beds also dry out faster than garden beds and require frequent waterings. Water the bed whenever the top 2" to 4" of soil is dry (depending on the depth of your bed), and before you see the soil shrink away from the sides of the bed.

1 Outline a 3-ft. × 5-ft. area with stakes and string. Use a shovel to remove all the grass inside the area. Dig a flat, 2"-deep, 6"-wide trench around the inner perimeter of the stakes. Measure and mark one 54" piece and one 30" piece on four 8-ft. timbers.

2 Lay the first course of timbers in the trench. Level each corner, adjusting the soil as necessary. Measure, mark, and cut second course, staggering the joints. Place the second course on the first, and drill ³⁄₁₆" pilot holes near the ends. Drive in the 6" nails.

3 Place the third course over the second, repeating the staggered joints. Secure it with nails, offsetting the pilot holes to avoid the nails below. Drill 1" drainage holes every 2 ft. horizontally. Line the bed with landscape fabric, attaching it with roofing nails. Fill the bed with topsoil to within 4" of the top.

4 Tamp the soil lightly with a shovel. Add the plants, loosening the root balls before planting. Apply a 3" layer of mulch, and water the bed.

A rock garden is an attractive alternative to traditional lawns and garden beds. This garden has been planted with mosses. Small varieties of alpine plants are also good choices.

Building a Rock Garden

Rock gardens offer a good way to landscape difficult sites Sloped areas or sites with sandy soil, for instance, are unfavorable for traditional lawns but are ideal for rock gardens. A rock garden is also a good choice if you're looking for an alternative to traditional groundcovers and garden beds. Rock gardens traditionally feature hardy, alpine plant varieties that typically require only infrequent watering.

Building a rock garden requires excavating the site (preferably a sloping or terraced area) and preparing the soil, placing the rocks, and, finally planting. Moving and positioning large rocks is the most difficult task. If your rock garden site is large, consider hiring a landscape contractor to deliver and place the rocks for you.

Rock gardens will look most natural if they're built with stones that are all the same variety—or at least with stones that are similar in appearance. Using stone like that found in natural outcroppings in your area is a good idea. In a region with limestone bluffs, for example, building a rock garden with pieces of limestone will give your garden a pleasing, natural look. Or in regions near the shore, using smoothly weathered small boulders is a logical choice.

Common Rock-Garden Plants

Plant Name
Hens-and-Chicks
Snow-in-Summer
Coral bells
Sedum
Dianthus
Rock jasmine
Rockcress
Dwarf juniper
Yarrow

How to Build a Rock Garden

1 The best site for a rock garden is sloping or terraced, ideally with southeast exposure. It should be completely free of deep-rooted weeds. If no such space is available, build up a raised bed with southeast exposure. The alpine plants traditionally used in rock gardens require nonclayey soil, with excellent drainage. If the existing soil is clayey, remove any groundcover and excavate the site to a depth of around 18". Replace the soil with equal parts loam, peat moss, and coarse sand.

2 Choose rocks that are indigenous to your area and of similar type. Porous rocks, like limestone, weather best. Rocks should be proportional in size to the site. Very large sites will require very large rocks. Begin at the base of the site, placing the most substantial stones first. The idea is to create the impression of a natural subterranean rock formation exposed by weathering. Set the stones in the soil so they are at least half buried and so their most weathered surfaces are exposed. Slightly less than half of the surface of the site should be rock. Avoid even spacing or rows of rocks. Once the rocks are in place, cover the soil with a mulch of complementary pea gravel or rock chips.

3 "New" rocks moved to the site will need to weather before they will look natural. Encourage weathering by promoting moss and lichen growth. In a blender, combine a handful of moss with a cup of buttermilk or yogurt. Paint the mixture on the exposed faces of rocks to promote moss growth.

4 After the rocks are in place for a few days and the soil has settled, begin planting the garden. As with the rocks, focus on native varieties and strive for natural placement, without excessive variety. You can plant several sizes, from small trees or shrubs to delicate alpine flowers. Place plants in crevices and niches between rocks, allowing them to cascade over the surface of the rock.

Paths & Patios

Pathways, garden steps and patios form the hallways and floors of outdoor living spaces. The building materials used for paths and patios serve more than just a functional purpose—they also contibute to the visual style of your landscape and so should be chosen carefully. The wood, stone, brick and concrete used in these projects should be chosen with an eye to how they will blend with your home's architecture and the other features in your yard.

• **Building garden steps** (pages 108, 110).

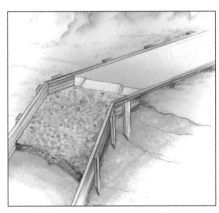

• **Building a concrete walkway** (page 114).

• **Installing a loose-fill pathway** (page 118).

• **Building a flagstone walkway** (page 120).

• **Building a boardwalk** (page 122).

• **Building a brick patio** (page 124).

• **Laying a concrete patio** (page 128).

• **Tiling a patio slab** (page 130).

107

How to Build Garden Steps (continued)

7 Excavate and install the remaining steps in the run. The back of the last step should be flush with the ground at the top of the slope. Staple plastic over the timbers to protect them while the concrete is being poured.

8 Cut away the plastic from the frame openings. Pour a 2" layer of compactible gravel into each frame, and use a scrap 2 × 4 to smooth it out.

9 Mix concrete and shovel it into the bottom frame, flush with the top of the timbers. Work the concrete lightly with a garden rake to help remove air bubbles, but don't overwork it. Screed the concrete smooth by dragging a 2 × 4 across the top of the frame. If necessary, add concrete to the low areas and screed the surface again until it is smooth and free of low spots. Use an edging tool to smooth the cracks between the concrete and the timbers. Pour concrete into the remaining steps, screeding and edging each step before moving on to the next.

10 While the concrete is still wet, create a textured, nonskid surface by drawing a clean, stiff-bristled broom across its surface in one sweeping motion. Remove the plastic from around the timbers. When the concrete has hardened, mist it with water, cover it with plastic, and let it cure for one week.

Garden Steps Variations

© Michael S. Thompson

Timbers & brick pavers offer interesting texture and pattern to a landscape. Construction is similar as to the timber and concrete project shown on the preceding pages.

Concrete & natural stone create an elegant and uniform walkway for a gentle slope.

Flagstone steps create a rustic pathway in a natural garden setting.

© This and center photograph by Jerry Pavia

Curving wood steps echo the informal tone of the rest of this landscape.

Brick steps are ideal in homes and landscapes with a classic or traditional style.

Precast concrete step forms make it easy to build a durable outdoor staircase. By overlapping the forms in varying arrangements, you can shape a staircase with curves, angles, and even spirals. Lay two forms side-by-side to create larger steps.

Building Steps with Cast Forms

An easy variation of garden steps (page 108) is to build them with precast concrete step forms. The forms are somewhat heavy but are otherwise easy to use and can be used to contain poured concrete, loose fill materials, or brick pavers, as shown here. Many manufacturers sell pavers that are sized to fit inside the forms they make. Decide how many forms you'll need for the steps you plan to build and the paver pattern you wish to use, then consult the manufacturer's specifications to determine the number of pavers required.

To plan the layout for this project, follow Steps 1 to 4 on page 108. You can adjust the amount of overlap for each step to fit the dimensions of your site or to create a desired appearance.

Everything You Need

Tools: Mason's string, drill, level, shovel, rake, hand tamper, tape measure, rubber mallet, broom.

Materials: Straight 2 × 4 board, stakes, screws, concrete step forms, pavers, compactible gravel, sand.

How to Build Steps with Cast Forms

1 Mark the outline of your steps with stakes and string, then excavate for the first step. Dig a hole 6" deeper than the height of the step and 4" wider and longer than the step on all sides.

2 Fill the hole with compactible gravel. Rake the gravel to create a slight downward slope (⅛" per foot) from back to front, for drainage. Tamp it well with a hand tamper, then set the first form in place. Use a level to make sure the form is level from side to side and has the proper slope from back to front.

3 Add a layer of gravel inside the form and tamp it well. The distance between the gravel and the top of the form should equal the thickness of a paver plus 1". Next, add a 1"-thick layer of sand over the gravel. Use a 2 × 4 set across the form to measure as you go.

4 Lay the pavers in the form in the desired pattern, keeping them level with the top of the form. Adjust as needed, using a rubber mallet or by adding sand underneath. Use a broom to spread sand over the pavers to fill the joints.

5 Excavate for the next step, accounting for the overlap and a 4" space behind and at the sides for gravel. Fill and tamp the gravel so the front is level with the top of the first step. Repeat Steps 2 to 4. When all steps are installed, backfill with dirt along the sides.

Building a Concrete Walkway

Pouring a sidewalk is a basic masonry project that teaches the skills needed for larger landscape projects, like pouring driveways and patios.

One key to success is to precisely build sturdy forms that have the proper slope for drainage. The forms are what contain and control the poured concrete, and the forms largely determine the quality of your project.

Finishing the poured concrete is another important step. Timing is key. After the concrete is poured, the heavy materials gradually sink, leaving a thin layer of water—known as bleed water—on the surface. It's important to screed the concrete and add control joints before the bleed water appears. Let the bleed water dry before floating or edging the concrete.

Everything You Need

Tools: Line level, hammer, shovel, sod cutter, wheelbarrow, tamper, drill, level, screed board, straightedge, mason's string, mason's float, mason's trowel, edger, groover, stiff-bristle broom.

Materials: Garden stakes, rebar, bolsters, 2 × 4 lumber, 1½" and 3" screws, concrete mix, concrete sealer, isolation board compactible gravel, construction adhesive, nails.

Tip:

Make a story pole to help you create a uniform excavation for your sidewalk. Mark the story pole at a distance equal to the distance from the string slope line you establish to the top of planned sidewalk, plus the thickness of your forms (usually 3½"), plus 4" for the gravel subbase. If your string line is 6" above ground level, for instance, your story pole should be at 13½" (6" plus 3½" plus 4"). As you dig, use the mark on the story pole to gauge the depth of the excavation.

How to Build a Concrete Walkway

1 Select a rough layout, including any turns. Stake out the location and connect the stakes with mason's strings, leveling them with a line level as you go. Set the slope of the slab to direct water runoff by lowering the height of the strings in the direction you want the water to go. A standard slope is $\frac{1}{8}$" of drop per foot of length in the strings. Remove the sod between and 6" beyond the lines and excavate the site to a depth 4" greater than the thickness of the slab.

2 Pour a 5" layer of compactible gravel as a subbase for the walkway. Tamp the subbase until it compacts to an even 4"-thick layer. The subbase should extend at least 6" beyond the project outline.

3 Cut 2 × 4s to length to use as forms for the walkway. Miter the ends to follow any turns. Use the mason's strings as a reference for setting the forms in place. Cut 12" stakes from 2 × 4s and drive them at 3-ft. intervals with a hand maul to support the forms.

4 Drive 2" deck screws through the stakes and into the forms on one side of the walkway. Use a level to guide you as you screw the form on the other side in place. Use construction adhesive to glue isolation board to any structure that adjoins the walkway.

(continued next page)

How to Build a Concrete Walkway (continued)

5 Coat the inside edges of the forms with vegetable oil. Mix concrete according to the manufacturer's instructions and pour it into the project area with a wheelbarrow. Use a masonry hoe to spread it evenly within the forms. Work a spade along the inside edges of the forms to remove any trapped air bubbles.

6 Rap the forms with a hammer to help settle the concrete. This also draws finer aggregates against the forms, creating a smoother surface on the sides.

7 Screed the pour before bleed water appears. Move the board in a side-to-side motion. Keep the screed flat to remove high spots and add concrete to low areas.

8 Before bleed water appears, cut control joints at intervals roughly 1½ times the walkway's width with a mason's trowel. Use a straight 2 x 4 as a guide. Control joints control where cracks occur in the future as natural settling occurs.

116

9 Wait until the bleed water disappears and float the area smooth with a long, arching motion. Do not overwork the surface. Stop floating if the bleed water reappears and resume when it is gone.

10 After floating the surface smooth, draw a groover along the control joints and around the perimeter of the walkway. Use a straight 2 × 4 as a guide for the control joints and float out any marks left by the grooving tool.

11 Create a nonskid surface by drawing a clean stiff-bristle broom across the walkway. Avoid overlapping the broom marks. Cover the walkway with plastic and let it cure for one week.

12 Remove the forms and backfill the sides of the walkway with dirt or sod. Seal the concrete if desired, according to the manufacturer's directions.

Flagstone walkways combine durability with beauty and work well for casual or formal landscapes.

Building a Flagstone Walkway

Natural flagstone is an ideal material for creating landscape floors. It's attractive and durable and blends well with both formal and informal landscapes. Although flagstone structures are often mortared, they can also be constructed with the sand-set method. Sand-setting flagstones is much faster and easier than setting them with mortar.

There are a variety of flat, thin sedimentary rocks that can be used for this project. Home and garden stores often carry several types of flagstone, but stone supply yards usually have a greater variety. Some varieties of flagstone cost more than others, but there are many affordable options. When you buy the flagstone for your project, select pieces in a variety of sizes from large to small. Arranging the stones for your walkway is similar to putting together a puzzle, and you'll need to see all the pieces laid out.

The following example demonstrates how to build a straight flagstone walkway with wood edging. If you'd like to build a curved walkway, select another edging material, such as brick or cut stone. Instead of filling gaps between stones with sand, you might want to fill them with topsoil and plant grass or some other ground cover between the stones.

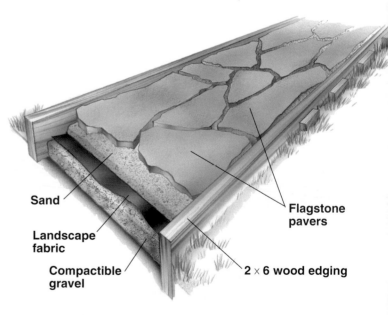

Sand

Landscape fabric

Compactible gravel

Flagstone pavers

2 × 6 wood edging

Everything You Need

Tools: Basic tools, line level, hand tamper, circular saw with masonry blade, power drill, masonry chisel, maul, rubber mallet, sod cutter (optional).

Materials: Landscape fabric, sand, 2 × 6 pressure-treated lumber, galvanized screws, compactible gravel, flagstone pavers, water.

How to Build a Flagstone Walkway

1 Lay out, excavate, and prepare the base for the walkway. Form edging by installing 2 × 6 pressure-treated lumber around the perimeter of the pathway. Drive stakes on the outside of the edging, spaced 12" apart. The tops of the stakes should be below ground level. Drive galvanized screws through the edging and into the stakes.

2 Test-fit the stones over the walkway base, finding an attractive arrangement that limits the number of cuts needed. The gaps between the stones should range between ⅜" and 2" wide. Use a pencil to mark the stones for cutting, then remove the stones and place them beside the walkway in the same arrangement. Score along the marked lines with a circular saw and masonry blade set to ⅛" blade depth. Set a piece of wood under the stone, just inside the scored line. Use a masonry chisel and hammer to strike along the scored line until the stone breaks.

3 If not planting grass, lay overlapping strips of landscape fabric over the walkway base and spread a 2" layer of sand over it. Make a screed board from a short 2 × 6, notched to fit inside the edging. Pull the screed from one end of the walkway to the other, adding sand as needed to create a level base.

4 Beginning at one corner of the walkway, lay the flagstones onto the sand base. Repeat the arrangement you created in Step 2, with ⅜"- to 2"-wide gaps between stones. If necessary, add or remove sand to level the stones, then set them by tapping them with a rubber mallet or a length of 2 × 4.

5 Fill the gaps between the stones with sand. (Use topsoil, if you're going to plant grass or ground cover between the stones.) Pack sand into the gaps, then spray the entire walkway with water to help settle the sand. Repeat until the gaps are completely filled and tightly packed with sand.

Building a Boardwalk

A boardwalk can be a good alternative to a traditional concrete sidewalk. Relatively inexpensive and easy to construct, a boardwalk can add a touch of elegance to any yard.

The project uses a very simple modular design that can be easily adapted to any circumstance. Frames measuring 29 × 45" are constructed from pressure-treated lumber and recessed in trenches along the project area. Cedar decking covers the frame. You could also use composite lumber products as the boardwalk surface. To ensure stability, fasten the frames together with lag screws driven through both sides of the end boards.

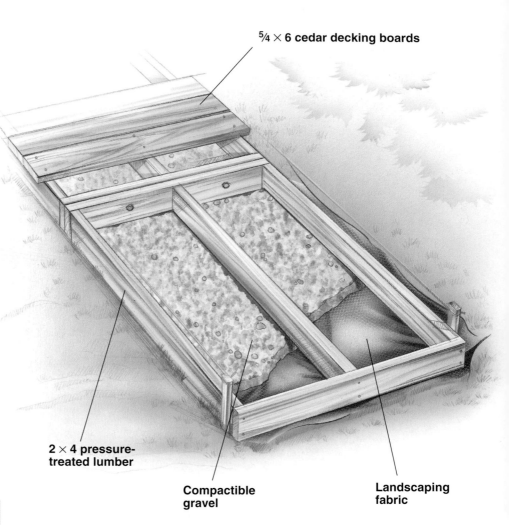

⁵⁄₄ × 6 cedar decking boards

2 × 4 pressure-treated lumber

Compactible gravel

Landscaping fabric

Cutting List

Dimensions for one panel:

Part	Type	Size	Qty.
Stringers	2 × 4	42"	3
End boards	2 × 4	29"	2
Decking	⁵⁄₄ × 6	32"	*

*as needed

Everything You Need

Tools: Tape measure, stakes & string, wheelbarrow, shovel, rake, hand tamper, framing square, circular saw, power drill, clamps, ratchet wrench, T-bevel.

Materials: Landscaping fabric, compactible gravel, 2 × 4 pressure-treated lumber, 2½" & 3" galvanized deck screws, ⁵⁄₁₆ × 2½" galvanized lag screws with washers, ⁵⁄₄ × 6 cedar decking boards.

How to Build a Boardwalk

1 Lay out the boardwalk site, using stakes and strings. Dig a trench 4½" deep and 34" wide to the length of the site. Line the base of the trench with strips of landscaping fabric, overlapping the strips by 6". Lay a 2" subbase of compactible gravel over the landscaping fabric. Use a hand tamper to pack the gravel into a firm, even surface.

2 The boardwalk is constructed as a series of frames attached to one another. For each frame, cut pressure-treated 2 × 4s as follows: three 42" boards (stringers) and two 29" boards (ends). Centered on the face of each end board (14½ from each end), drill a pair of ¹⁄₁₆" pilot holes. Put a hole approximately ¾" from each edge. Lay out the pieces on a flat surface. Butt the ends of the stringers against the end boards, with the side stringers flush with the ends of the end boards and the middle stringer aligned with the pilot holes at the midpoint. Fasten the pieces together, using 3" galvanized deck screws and checking for square with a framing square. Build as many frames as needed to cover the boardwalk site. For sections shorter than 42", cut the stringers for the last frame 3" shorter than the remaining length to allow for the width of the end boards.

3 Butt frames end-to-end in the trench. Clamp together and drill four ³⁄₁₆" pilot holes in the end boards, one between each pair of stringers, on both sides of the end boards. Fasten with ⁵⁄₁₆ × 2½" galvanized lag screws with washers, using a ratchet wrench. Backfill the space between the outside edge of the stringers and the trench with compactible gravel for drainage.

4 Cut ⁵⁄₄ × 6" decking boards to 32", using a circular or handsaw. Starting at one end, center a decking board on the frame so there is a 1½" overhang on each side. Drill pairs of ¹⁄₁₆" pilot holes in the board at each stringer location, and attach the decking to the frames, using 2½" galvanized deck screws. Repeat, keeping ¼" spaces between boards. If needed, rip the final decking board to size at the end of the boardwalk.

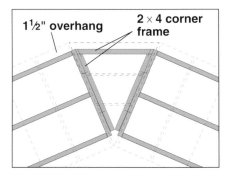

Variation: To create a corner, position two frame sections at the angle in the trench with the front corners touching. Tack a string between the back corners, then measure and cut pressure-treated 2 × 4s to size for one corner stringer and two nailers. Use a T-bevel to find the angles created by the turn, and miter-cut the ends of each board to the angle of the turn. Fasten the pieces together with 3" deck screws. For the decking, use the same angle to miter-cut across the face of the boards. Cut them to size as you go.

Building a Brick Patio

Brick pavers are versatile and durable, and they come in a variety of shapes, patterns, and colors, making them an excellent material for creating walkways and patios. They convey an impression of formality, quickly dressing up your landscape. It's best to use concrete pavers rather than traditional clay bricks, as concrete pavers have self-spacing lugs that make them easy to install. See page 16 to estimate pavers.

The easiest way to build a patio or walkway with brick pavers is to set them in sand. With this method, the pavers rest on a 1" layer of sand spread over a prepared base. Pavers are then arranged over the sand, and the joints between them are densely packed with more sand. The sand keeps the pavers in place, but it still allows them to shift as the ground contracts and expands with temperature changes.

Everything You Need

Tools: Tape measure, carpenter's level, shovel, line level, rake, hand tamper, tamping machine.

Materials: Stakes, mason's string, compactible gravel subbase, rigid plastic edging, landscape fabric, sand, pavers, 1"-thick pipes.

How to Build a Sand-set Patio with Brick Pavers

1 Lay out and excavate for the patio, using the same techniques as for a concrete walkway (page 114). Cut strips of landscape fabric and lay them over the base, overlapping each strip by at least 6". Install rigid plastic edging around the edges of the patio, anchored with galvanized spikes (inset). For curves and rounded patio corners, use rigid edging with notches on the outside flange (inset).

2 Remove strings, then place 1"-thick pipes or wood strips over the landscape fabric, spaced every 6 ft. to serve as depth spacers for laying the sand base.

124

3 Spread a 1" layer of sand over the landscape fabric, using a garden rake to smooth it out. The sand should just cover the tops of the depth spacers. Water the layer of sand thoroughly, then lightly pack it down with a hand tampe.

4 Screed the sand to an even layer by resting a long 2 × 4 on the spacers and drawing it across the sand, using a sawing motion. Fill footprints and low areas with sand, then water, tamp, and screed again.

5 Lay the first border paver in one corner of the patio, making sure it rests firmly against the plastic edging. Lay the next paver snug against the first. Set the pavers by tapping them into the sand with a mallet. Use the depth of the first paver as a guide for setting the remaining pavers in a 2-ft. section.

6 After each section is set, use a long level to make sure the pavers are flat. Make adjustments by tapping high pavers deeper into the sand, or by removing low pavers and adding a thin layer of additional sand underneath them.

(continued next page)

How to Build a Sand-set Patio with Brick Pavers (continued)

7 Continue installing 2-ft.-wide sections of the border and interior pavers. At rounded corners, install border pavers in a fan pattern with even gaps between the pavers. Gentle curves may accommodate full-sized border pavers, but for sharper bends, you'll need to mark and cut wedge-shaped border pavers to fit. Use a circular saw with a masonry blade to cut the pavers. Lay the remaining interior pavers.

8 Use a 2 × 4 to check that the entire patio is flat. Adjust any uneven pavers by tapping them with the mallet or by adding more sand beneath them.

9 Spread a ½" layer of sand over the patio, then use the tamping machine to compress the entire patio and pack the sand into the joints.

10 Sweep up the loose sand, then soak the patio area thoroughly to settle the sand in the joints. Let the surface dry completely. If necessary, spread and pack sand over the patio again, until all the joints are tightly packed.

Installation Variations for Brick Pavers

Dry mortar: (Shown at right) Installation is similar to sand-set patio, but joints are ⅜" wide and are packed with a mixture of sand and mortar, soaked with water, and finished with a jointing tool. A dry-mortar patio has a more finished masonry look than a sand-set patio, but the joints must be repaired periodically.

Wet mortar: This method often is used when pavers are installed over an old concrete patio or sidewalk. Pavers can be laid in much the same fasion as stone tiles over a concrete patio slab (see page 130). Joints are ½" wide. Wet mortar installation can also be used with flagstone. For edging on a wet-mortar patio, use rigid plastic edging or paver bricks set on end.

After the mortar has been packed into the joints and wetted, finish the joints with a jointing tool.

Common Paving Patterns for Standard Brick Pavers

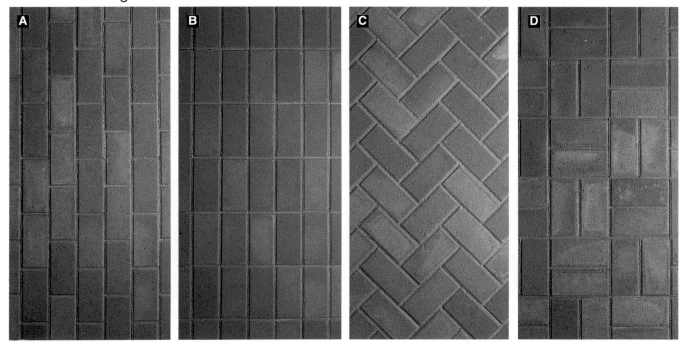

Standard brick pavers can be arranged in several different patterns, including: (A) running bond, (B) jack-on-jack, (C) herringbone, and (D) basket-weave. Jack-on-jack and basketweave patterns require fewer cut pavers along the edges. Standard pavers have spacing lugs on the sides that automatically set the joints at the right width.

127

Stone tiles can be laid as veneer over a concrete patio slab—a very easy way to create an elegant looking patio.

Tiling a Patio Slab

Outdoor tile can be made of several different materials and is available in many colors and styles. A popular current trend is to use natural stone tiles with different shapes and complementary colors, as demonstrated in this project. Tile manufacturers may offer brochures giving you ideas for modular patterns that can be created from their tiles. Make sure the tiles you select are intended for outdoor use.

When laying a modular, geometric pattern with tiles of different sizes, it's crucial that you test the layout before you begin and that you place the first tiles very carefullly. The first tiles will dictate the placement of all other tiles in your layout.

You can pour a new masonry slab on which to install your tile patio (page 128), but another option is to finish an existing slab by veneering it with tile—the scenario demonstrated here.

Outdoor tile must be installed on a clean, flat and stable surface When tiling an existing con-

crete pad, the surface must be free of flaking, wide cracks, and other major imperfections. A damaged slab can be repaired by applying a 1- to 2"-thick layer of new concrete over the old surface before laying tile.

Note: Wear eye protection when cutting tile and handle cut tiles carefully—the cut edges of some materials may be very sharp.

Everything You Need

Tools: Tape measure, pencil, chalk line, tile cutter or wet saw, tile nippers, square-notched trowel, 2 × 4 padded with carpet, hammer, grout float, grout sponge, caulk gun.

Materials: Tile spacers, buckets, paintbrush and roller, plastic sheeting, thin-set mortar, modular tile, grout, grout additive, grout sealer, tile sealer.

Tile options for landscape installations: Slate and other smooth, natural stone materials are durable and blend well with any landscape but are usually expensive. Quarry tile is less expensive, though only available in limited colors. Exterior-rated porcelain or ceramic tiles are moderately priced and available in a wide range of colors and textures, with many styles imitating the look of natural stone. Terra cotta tile is made from molded clay for use in warmer, drier climates only. Many of these materials require application of a sealer to increase durability and prevent staining and moisture penetration.

Tools for installing exterior tile include: a wet saw for cutting tile quickly and easily (available at rental centers—make certain to rent one that is big enough for the tile size you install), an angle grinder with a diamond-edged cutting blade (also a rental item) for cutting curves or other complex contours, a trowel with square notches (of the size required for your tile size) for spreading the mortar adhesive, spacers for accurate aligning of tiles and setting consistent joint widths, a straight length of 2 x 4 padded along one edge (carpet pad works well) for helping align tile surfaces, a grout float for spreading grout to fill the joints, and a sponge for cleaning excess grout from tile surfaces.

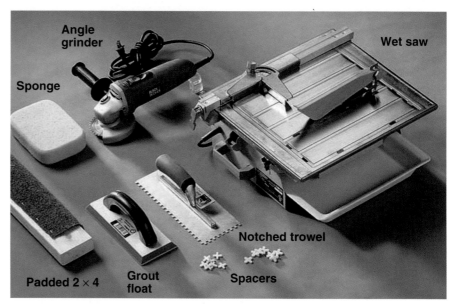

Materials for installing exterior tile include: latex-modified thin-set mortar adhesive that is mixed with water (if you can't find thin-set that is latex modified, buy unmodified thin-set and mix it with a latex additive for mortar, following manufacturer's directions), exterior-rated grout available in a variety of colors to match the tile you use, grout additive to improve durability, grout sealer to help protect grout from moisture and staining, and tile sealer required for some tile materials (follow tile manufacturer's requirements).

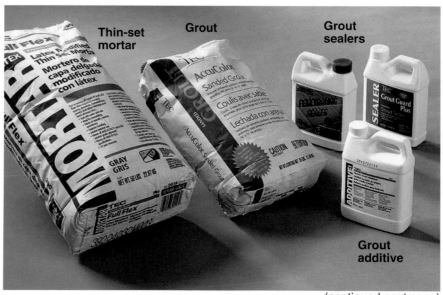

(continued next page)

Variation: To establish a traditional grid pattern, test-fit rows of tiles so they run in each direction, intersecting at the center of the patio. Adjust the layout to minimize tile cutting at the sides and ends, then mark the final layout and snap chalklines across the patio to create four quadrants. As you lay tile, work along the chalklines and in one quadrant at a time.

3 Following manufacturer's instructions, mix enough thin-set mortar to work for about 2 hours (start with 4 to 5" deep in a 5-gallon bucket. At the intersection of the two layout lines, use a notched-edge trowel to spread thin-set mortar over an area large enough to accommodate the layout of the first modular group of tiles. Hold the trowel at a 45° angle to rake the mortar to a consistent depth.

4 Set the first tile, twisting it slightly as you push it into the mortar. Align it with both adjusted layout lines, then place a padded 2 × 4 over the center of the tile and give it a light rap with a hammer to set the tile.

5 Position the second tile adjacent to the first with a slight gap between them. Place spacers on end in the joint near each corner and push the second tile against the spacers. Make certain the first tile remains aligned with the layout lines. Set the padded 2 × 4 across both tiles and tap to set. Use a damp cloth to remove any mortar that squeezes out of the joint or gets on tile surfaces. Joints must be at least ⅛"-deep to hold grout.

6 Lay the remaining tiles of the first modular unit, using spacers. Using the trowel, scrape the excess mortar from the concrete pad in areas you will not yet be working to prevent it from hardening and interfering with tile installation.

7 With the first modular unit set, continue laying tile following the pattern established. You can use the chalklines for general reference, but they will not be necessary as layout lines. To prevent squeeze-out between tiles, scrape a heavy accumulation of mortar ½" away from the edge of a set tile before setting the adjacent tile.

Tip: Cutting Contours in Tile

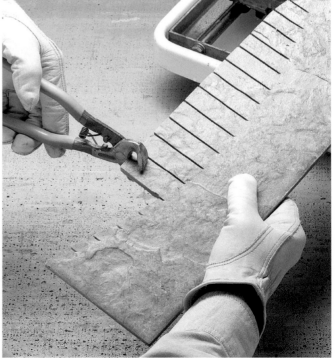

To make convex (left) or concave (right) curves, mark the profile of the curve on the tile, then use a wet saw to make parallel straight cuts, each time cutting as close to the marked line as possible. Use a tile noppers to break off small portions of tabs, gradually working down to the curve profile. Finally, use an angle grinder to smooth off the sharp edges of the tabs. Make sure to wear a particle mask when using the tile saw and wear sturdy gloves when using the nippers.

(continued next page)

Fences & Garden Walls

In this section, you'll find detailed, easy-to-follow instructions for all the fence and garden wall projects shown below.

As is true for many of the features inside your home, outdoor fences and walls are not only functional, but decorative, as well. Carefully consider your choices of materials with an eye to their visual appeal in the landscape.

- **Building a panel fence** (page 150).
- **Building a board & stringer fence** (page 152).

- **Building a picket fence** (page 154).
- **Building a post & rail fence** (page 156).

- **Building a vinyl fence** (page 160).

- **Building a chain-link fence** (page 164).

- **Building a custom gate** (page 168).
- **Building an arbor gate** (page 172).

- **Building brick pillars** (page 178).
- **Building a brick & cedar fence** (page 182).

- **Building a brick archway** (page 184).

- **Building a concrete block garden wall** (page 188).

- **Building a dry stone wall** (page 192).

Basic Techniques for Building Fences & Garden Walls

A good fence or garden wall begins with carefully plotting the location of the structure, first on a site map drawing of your yard (page 27), then tranferring this layout to the yard itself. Most fences and garden walls are built with straight lines and angles, but a curved wall can add appeal to an otherwise ordinary landscape. On the following introductory pages, you'll find simple methods for laying out both straight and curved lines for walls and fences.

It's pretty easy to plot and build a fence when the ground is perfectly flat and level, but it gets a bit more complicated when your yard includes hills, slight valleys, or consistent downward grades. The opening pages on basic construction show two common ways to handle the problem of slope: contouring and stepping.

A contoured fence is the easier of the two solutions. The stringers between the posts run roughly parallel with the ground, so the fence remains at consistent height and rolls in unison with the terrain. Contouring works best over large areas of slope, with post-and-rail or picket fences.

A stepped fence takes more time and effort but creates a more structured look. Each section between posts "steps" down in equal increments, creating a uniform fence line. Stepping works best over gradual slopes. Steep hills or valleys rise too much over short runs and will cause large gaps between the ground and the bottom of the fence.

Whichever method you use, make sure your posts are plumb and properly set in the ground. If they are not, gravity will work on your fence line and create structural problems over time.

A freestanding garden wall serves the same function as a fence, but it is much sturdier and requires footings rather than posts. Footings provide a stable, level base for brick, block, stone, and poured concrete structures. They distribute the weight of the structure evenly, prevent sinking, and keep structures from moving during seasonal freeze-thaw cycles. Limit your walls to 3 ft. in height. Taller walls need deep footings and extra reinforcement.

Everything You Need:

Tools: Basic tools (page 18), plumb bob, stakes, hand maul, power auger or posthole digger, shovel, level, mason's trowel, rope or hose, rake,

Materials: Pressure-treated, cedar, or redwood 4 × 4 and 2 × 6 lumber, scrap lengths of 2 × 4, compactible gravel subbase, #3 rebar/tie rods, 16-gauge wire, vegetable oil, premixed concrete, sheet plastic, mason's string.

How to Plot a Straight Fence Line

1 Plan your fence line with a setback of at least 6" from the legal property line. (Local regulations may require a larger setback.) Draw a detailed site map, taking all aspects of your landscape into consideration, with the location of each post accurately marked. Mark the fence line with stakes at each end or corner post location, and mason's string between. Adjust the string until it is level, using a line level as a guide.

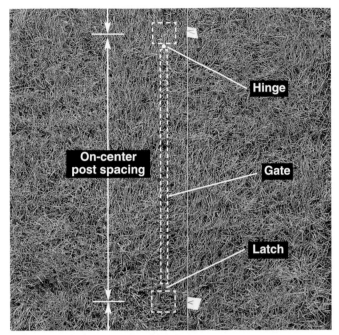

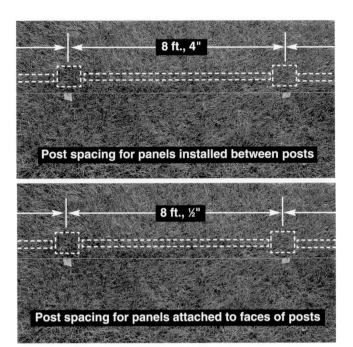

2 To find the on-center spacing for the gate posts, combine the width of the gate and the clearance necessary for the hinges and latch hardware, then add 4". Mark the string with masking tape to indicate where the gate posts will be installed.

3 Refer to your site map, and then measure and mark the line post locations on the string, using masking tape. Remember that the tape indicates the center of the post, not the edge.

How to Plot a Right Angle

1 Begin marking the fence line with stakes and mason's string. At the location of the outside corner, plant a stake. Connect the corner stake to the previous stake with mason's string. Plant another stake exactly 3 ft. from the corner stake along the line.

2 Position the end of one tape measure at the outside corner of the last two stakes. Open the tape on the corner stake past the 4 ft. mark and lock it. Open the other tape past the 5 ft. mark and lock it. Now have a helper adjust the two tape meaasures until the 5 ft. measurement and the 4 ft. markings intersect. At this point, drive another stake and attach another mason's string extending from the corner post through the new stake. The line formed by this stake and the corner stake will be at an exact 90° angle to the first fence line.

How to Plot a Curve

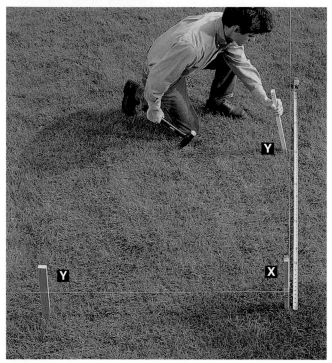

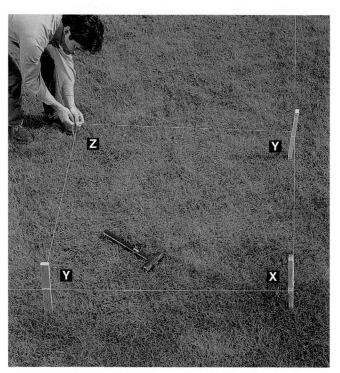

1 Plot a right angle, using the 3-4-5 triangle method (page 141). Measure and plant stakes equidistant from the outside corner (X) to mark the end points for the curve (Y).

2 To create a compass, tie a mason's string to each end stake and extend the strings back to the corner stake. Then hold them tight at the point where they meet. Pull out this point, opposite the corner stake, until the strings are taut. Plant a stake (Z) at this point to complete a square.

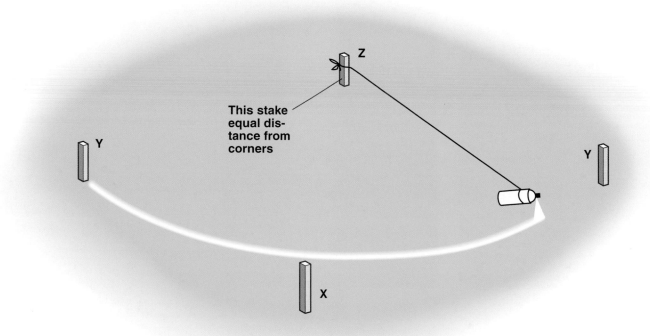

This stake equal distance from corners

3 To mark the curve, tie a mason's string to the stake (Z), just long enough to reach the end points of the curve (Y). Pull the string taut and hold a can of spray paint at the end of it. Moving in an arc between the end points, spray paint the curve on the ground.

How to Contour a Fence for a Slope

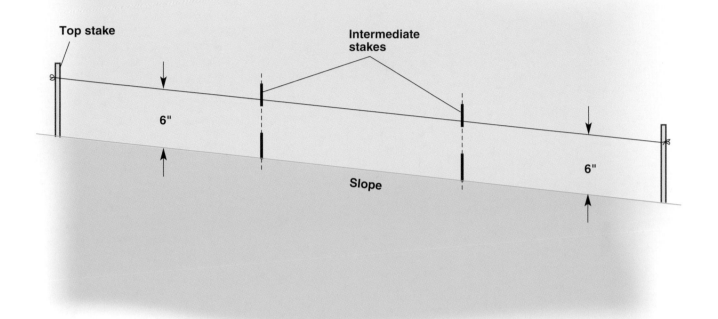

Top stake

Intermediate stakes

6"

6"

Slope

1 Outline the fence location with stakes and string, as shown on pages 140 to 141. Drive one stake into the ground at the top of the slope and one at the bottom. Make sure the stakes are plumb. Run string between the stakes, 6" above the ground at each stake. Measure and mark equidistant post locations along the string, using pieces of tape. Drop a plumb bob from each piece of tape and mark the ground with a stake for the post-hole location.

2 Dig footings and set the posts in concrete (page146 to 147). Allow to cure for two days. Measure up from the base of each post and mark cutoff lines for the height, using a framing square. Trim the posts along the cutoff lines, using a reciprocating saw or handsaw. Each post will be the same height, creating a contour fence line that follows any ground variance you may find on your property.

(continued next page)

How to Contour a Fence for a Slope (continued)

3 On each post, measure down from the top, and mark a line for both the upper and lower stringer positions. Clamp a board for the upper stringer between two posts, aligning the top edge with the upper stringer reference marks of each. Scribe each post outline on the backside of the stringer. Remove the stringer and cut it to size, using a circular saw. Position the stringer between the two posts and toenail it into place, using galvanized nails or deck screws. Repeat this process to install the remaining stringers, both upper and lower, in their proper positions. Apply the siding. Mark each board with a reference line, so each will extend evenly above the upper stringer. If necessary, trim the bottoms to maintain 2" of clearance from the ground. Use spacers between the boards to maintain consistent spacing.

How to Step a Fence

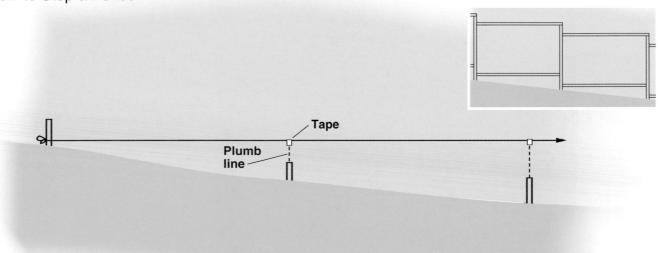

1 Drive a short stake into the ground at the top of the slope and a longer stake at the bottom. Make sure the top of the longer stake rises above the bottom of the shorter stake. Check the longer stake for plumb with a level. Run string from the bottom of the short stake to the top of the longer one. Using a line level, adjust the string at the longer stake until it is level and mark the position. Measure the length of the string from stake to stake. This number is the run. Divide the run into equal segments that are between 48" and 96". This will give you the number of sections and posts

(number of sections + 1) you will need. Example: 288" (run) ÷ 72" (section size) = 4 (number of sections). Measure the longer stake from the ground to the string mark for the rise. Divide the rise by the number of sections you will have on the slope for the stepping measurement. Example: 24" (rise) ÷ 4 (sections between posts) = 6" (step size). Measure and mark the post locations along the level string with a piece of tape. Drop a plumb bob from each post location mark on the string and mark the ground with a stake.

144

2 Dig the postholes and set the posts (pages 140 to 141). Allow the concrete to cure for two days. On the post at the bottom of the slope, measure up from the ground and mark the post height. Cut the post at the mark, using a reciprocating saw or handsaw. Use a line level to run a level string from the top of this post to the next post. Mark a reference line on the post. Measure up from this reference line and mark the step size (6" in our example). Cut the post to size with a reciprocating saw or handsaw. Measure down from the reference line and mark the lower stringer position, repeating for each post, until you reach the top of the slope.

3 Measure across the top of the post to the reference line on the next post. Cut the board for the upper stringer to size. Place the stringer with one end on the post top and the other flush against the next post at the reference mark. Make sure the stringer is level and attach it, using 3" galvanized deck screws. Measure the distance between the posts and cut the boards for the lower stringers to size. Continue this process until you reach the top of the slope. Apply the siding. Mark each board with a reference line so each will extend evenly above the upper stringer. If necessary, trim the bottoms so they're even below the lower stringer. Use spacers between the boards to maintain consistent spacing.

145

1 Lay out the position of the wall, using a rope or hose, then use stakes and mason's string to outline footings that are twice as wide as the proposed project and extend 1 ft. beyond each end. Make sure the outline is square, using a framing square.

2 Strip away sod 6" outside the project area on all sides, then excavate the trench for the footing to a depth of 12" below the frost line. The bottom of the trench should be roughly level. Lay a 6" layer of compactible gravel subbase into the trench and tamp thoroughly.

3 Build and install a 2 x 4 form frame to outline the footings, aligning the forms with mason's string. Drive stakes along the outside of the forms to anchor them into position, then adjust to level.

4 Make two #3 rebar grids to reinforce each footing. For each grid, use a reciprocating saw to cut (inset) two pieces of #3 rebar 8" shorter than the length of the footing and two pieces 4" shorter than the depth of the footing. For longer footings make many smaller grids to cover the greater spans. Bind the rebar pieces together with 16-gauge wire, forming a rectangle. Set the grids upright in the trench, leaving 4" of space between the grids and the walls of the trench. Coat the inside edges of the forms with vegetable oil or commercial release agent.

5 Make sure you have a clear path from your concrete source to your project area. Build a ramp from 2 x 6 lumber if necessary. Mix the concrete according to manufacturer's instructions. Remove air pockets by working the concrete with a shovel. Pour the concrete in evenly spaced loads, starting at the farthest end. Pour the concrete so it reaches the tops of the forms. Screed the surface of the concrete by dragging a short 2 x 4 along the top of the forms. Add concrete to any low areas that form. Screed the surface again and add tie-rods if needed. Float the concrete until it is smooth and level.

6 When the concrete is hard to the touch, cover with plastic and let cure for two to three days. Remove the forms and backfill around the edges of the footings. Add compactible gravel to bring the surrounding areas level with the surface of the footings. Let the footings cure for one week to maximize strength.

Variation: Add tie-rods if you will be pouring concrete over the footing. After the concrete sets up, press 12" sections of rebar 6" into the concrete. The tie-rods will anchor the footing to the structure it supports.

Building a Board & Stringer Fence

Dog-eared siding

Stringers

2" fence brackets

4 x 4 post

Footing

Gravel

GATE POST LAYOUT

Hinge

Gate hardware

On-center post spacing

Gate

Latch

If you want a high-quality, well-built wood fence, a board and stringer fence may be the best answer. This fence style is constructed from a basic frame with at least two rails, called stringers, that run parallel to the ground between posts to form the framework. Vertical boards, called siding, are attached to the framework created by the stringers.

A board and stringer fence is well-suited for yards of almost any contour. Consult the section on handling slope (page 143) for instructions on how to adapt a board & stringer fence to a sloped yard.

We used dog-eared siding in this project, but these construction methods can be used with many siding patterns (see Variations below). Spend a little time looking at magazines and driving through your favorite neighborhoods—you're certain to find a siding style that appeals to you and suits your property.

Variations: Board Patterns

Louvered

Lattice top

Staggered board

Stockade

Everything You Need:

Tools: Masonry tools (page 19), tape measure, chalk line, line level, reciprocating saw or handsaw, paintbrush, circular saw, hammer, drill, level, wood sealer/protectant or paint.

Materials: Pressure-treated, cedar, or redwood lumber; 4 × 4s, 10 ft.; 2 × 4s, 8 ft.; 1 × 6s, 8 ft.; 2" galvanized deck screws; galvanized 2 × 4 fence brackets; 4d galvanized box nails; 3" galvanized deck screws; 6d galvanized box nails; 1/8" piece of scrap wood; prefabricated gate & hardware; wood scraps for shims.

How to Build a Board and Stringer Fence

1 Lay out the fence line and install the posts (pages 140 to 147), letting the concrete cure two days. On each post, measure up from the ground to a point 12" below the planned fence height. Snap a level chalk line across all posts at this height.

2 Trim the posts, using a reciprocating saw. Brush sealer-preservative onto the cut ends of the posts, as well as the ends of all cut stringers, and let them dry.

3 Cut a 2 × 4 to 72" for the top stringer. Place the stringers flat on top of the posts, centering the joints over each post. Attach the stringers to the posts, using 3" galvanized deck screws

4 To install the remaining stringers, measure down from the top of each post, marking lines at 24" intervals. At each mark, attach a fence bracket to the inside face of the post, flush with the outside edge, using 4d box nails. Accommodate a slope by bending the bottom flanges of the brackets to match the angles of the stringers. Scribe the back side of stringers along the edges of the posts and cut stringers ¼" shorter than marked so they'll easily slide into the brackets. Position the stringers in the brackets and secure them with 6d galvanized box nails.

5 To install siding, measure from the ground to the top edge of the top stringer on an end post and add 8½". Cut a 1 × 6 to this length and seal its edges. Position the 1 × 6 so that its top extends 10½" above the top stringer, leaving a 2" gap at the bottom. Make sure the siding board is plumb, then attach it to the post and rails with pairs of 2" galvanized deck screws. Leave a gap of at least ⅛" between remaining siding boards, using pieces of scrap wood for spacers. If necessary, rip boards at the ends of the fence to make them fit.

6 Attach three hinges to the gate frame, evenly spaced and parallel to the gate edge. Shim the gate into position between the gate posts. Drill pilot holes and attach the hinges to the gate post, using the screws provided with the hinge hardware. Attach three hinges to the gate frame, evenly spaced and parallel to the gate edge. On the opposite side, attach the latch hardware to the fence and to the gate. Adjust latch if necessary. Paint or seal the fence.

©Charles Mann

Building a Picket Fence

The charm of a picket fence lies in its open and inviting appearance. The repetitive structure and spacing create a pleasing rhythm that welcomes family and friends while maintaining a fixed property division.

Traditionally, picket fences are 36" to 48" tall. Our version is 48" tall, the posts are spaced 96" on-center, and the pickets are spaced 1¾" apart. It's important that the spacing appear to be consistent. Using a jig simplifies that process, and if necessary, you can spread any extra space across many pickets to mask the discrepancy.

Picket fences are traditionally white; however, matching your house's trim color or stain can be an eye-catching alternative. You'll need to apply two coats of paint or stain. If you prime and paint all the materials before construction, apply a second coat after the fence is completed to cover any marks, smudges, and nail or screw heads.

There are a number of picket styles to choose from. Most building centers carry a variety, or you can design your own by simply creating a template. If you need a large quantity of pickets or want to use an intricate design, contact a cabinet shop in your area to create the pickets for you—the time saved may be worth the added expense.

Everything You Need:

Tools: Tools for setting posts (page 146), circular saw, jigsaw, paintbrush & roller, tape measure, reciprocating saw or handsaw, spring clamps, framing square, drill.

Materials: Pressure-treated, cedar, or redwood lumber: 1 × 4s, 8 ft. (9 per bay); 2 × 4s, 8 ft. (2 per bay); 4 × 4s, 8 ft. (2 per bay); paint, stain, or sealer; 16d galvanized nails; 1½" galvanized deck screws; fence post finials.

Cutting List

Each 96" bay requires:

Part	Type	Size	Qty.
Posts	4 × 4	78"	2
Pickets	1 × 4	46"	18
Stringers	2 × 4	92½"	2
Jig	1 × 4	1¾" × 46"	1

Tip for Spacing Pickets

Example:

18 (pickets) × 3½" (picket width) = 63" (total picket width)

92½" (space between posts) − 63" = 29½" (unoccupied space)

29½" ÷ 17 (18 pickets − 1) = 1¾" (space between pickets)

Note: Not all calculations will work out evenly. If your figures come out uneven, make slight adjustments across the entire fence section.

How to Build a Picket Fence

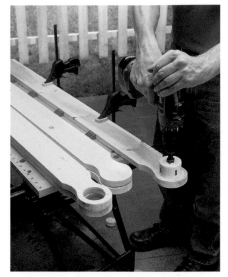

1 Lay out the fence line with stakes and mason's string. Space the post locations every 96" on-center. Count the 4 × 4 posts and estimate the number of pickets you'll need to complete the project, plus a few to compensate for any errors. If you're creating your own pickets, cut 1 × 4s to length. (Our design calls for 46" pickets.)

2 Set the posts. Allow the concrete footings to cure for two days. Measure up 48" from the base of each post and mark cutting lines. Trim the posts along the cutting lines, using a reciprocating saw or handsaw.

3 On each post, measure and mark a line 6" down from the top of the post to indicate the upper stringer position, and 36½" from the top to indicate the lower stringer. At the upper stringer marks on the first two posts, clamp an 8-ft. 2 × 4 with the top edge of the 2 × 4 flush with the mark. Scribe the post outline on the back of the stringer at each end.

4 Cut the upper stringer to size, using a circular saw. Position it between the two posts, set back ¾" from the face of the posts. Toenail the stringer into place with 16d galvanized nails.

5 Calculate the picket spacing and make a spacing jig by ripping a 1 × 4 to the spacing size—1¾" in this project. Draw a reference mark on each picket, 6" down from the peak. Position the first picket so the reference line is flush with the top edge of the upper stringer, drill pilot holes, and secure it with 1½" galvanized deck screws. Using the spacing jig, position and install the remaining pickets.

6 Attach fence post finials for detail. Use a straightedge to draw lines from corner to corner on the top of the post to determine the center. Drill a pilot hole where the lines intersect and screw a finial into the center of each post. For painted fences, apply a second coat.

Building a Post & Rail Fence

Post-and-rail construction can be used to build fences in a surprising range of styles, from a rustic split-rail fence to the more genteel post and rail fence, with or without a capped top.

Because they use so little lumber, split-rail fences are an inexpensive way to cover a large area of land. We show you how to build this fence by setting the posts in gravel-and-dirt footings. This method is common in some regions but isn't appropriate everywhere. You can set the posts in concrete (pages 146 to 147) if required by the building codes in your area.

One other note: if you don't want to cut mortises yourself, most lumberyards offer premortised posts and tapered stringers that can be used to build split-rail fences.

Post and rail fences, which typically are painted but sometimes are stained and sealed, require more lumber and more upkeep than split-rail fences but, in certain settings, nothing else will do. There are endless variations on rail placement, but the directions shown here will give you a good understanding of the basics involved. You should be able to adapt the plans and build just about any design that appeals to you.

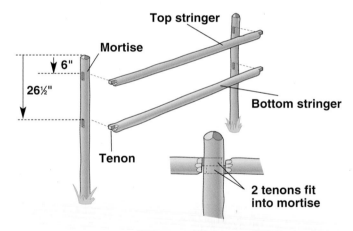

Everything You Need:

Tools: Cardboard, chalk line, shovel, combination square, drill, with 1"-bit, 2" wood chisel, chisel and hammer, reciprocating saw with a 6" wood blade, rubber mallet.

Materials: Lumber (see Cutting List), coarse gravel.

Cutting List

Each 72" bay requires:

Part	Type	Size	Qty.
Posts	4 × 4	66"	2
Stringers	4 × 4	72"	2

How to Build a Split-Rail Fence

1 Plot the fence line, spacing posts every 72" on center. Dig postholes. From the top of each post, measure and mark points 6" and 26½" down the center. Outline 2"-wide by 4"-tall mortises at each mark, using a cardboard template.

2 Drill a series of 1" holes inside each mortise outline, drilling through the backside if necessary. Drill only halfway through for end posts, and halfway through on adjacent sides for corner posts. Remove the remaining wood from the mortises with a hammer and chisel.

3 To make the tenons, snap a straight chalk line down the sides of the stringers. On one end, draw a straight line from the chalk line mark at the edge, using a combination square. At the center, draw a 1½"-long line perpendicular to the first, extending ¾" from each side. From each end of this line, draw perpendicular lines up to the edge of the timber. The result is a rough, 1½ × 1½"-square tenon end. Measure and mark 3½" down from the end for the tenon length. Cut the tenons with a reciprocating saw. Shape them with a hammer and chisel to fit the mortises.

4 Fill the postholes with 6" of gravel, and insert the first post. Because each post is cut to size, make sure the post top measures 36" from the ground. If it sits too high, lay a board over the post top and tap down with a rubber mallet. If it's too low, add more gravel. Leave 6" of clearance between the position of the bottom stringer and the ground. Fill the posthole with gravel and dirt, tamping down the dirt every few inches and checking the post for plumb. Place the next post in the posthole without setting it. Insert the tenons of the stringers into the mortises of the first set post. Insert the other ends of the stringers to the unset post. Adjust to fit. Plumb the post and set with a dirt and gravel footing. Repeat this procedure of setting a post, then attaching the stringers. Alternate the stringers so the tenons of one stringer face up and the tenons of the next stringer face down, creating a tight fit in the mortise. Plumb each post as you go.

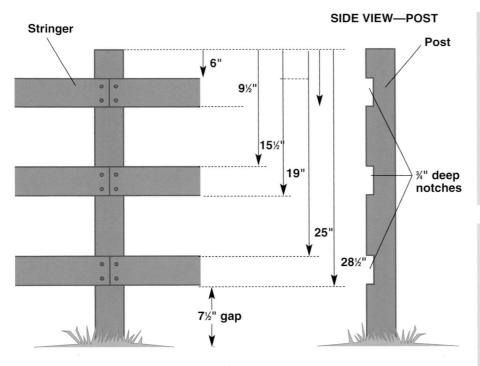

Stringer

SIDE VIEW—POST

Post

6"

9½"

15½"

19"

25"

28½"

¾" deep notches

7½" gap

Everything You Need:

Tools: Tools for setting posts (page 146), tape measure, bar clamps, circular saw, framing square, chisel & hammer, paintbrush & roller, stakes, line level, drill.

Materials: Lumber (see Cutting List), paint, stain, or sealer, 2" galvanized deck screws.

Cutting List

Each 72" bay requires:

Part	Type	Size	Qty.
Posts	4 × 4	66"	2
Stringers	1 × 4	72"*	3

*add 1¾" for end stringers

How to Build a Post & Rail Fence

1 Mark the fence line and dig postholes 72" on-center (pages 146 to 147). Cut 4 × 4 posts to 66". Measure and mark at 6", 9½", 15½", 19", 25", and 28½" down from the top of two posts. Gang several posts between the marked posts and clamp them together, using bar clamps. Use a framing square to extend the marks across all the posts. Mark the notches with an X between each pair of marks. Cut and finish all stringer lumber and let dry.

2 To notch the posts, make a series of cuts inside each set of reference lines, using a circular saw with the blade depth set at ¾". Remove the remaining wood in each notch, using a hammer and chisel. Remove wood only to the depth of the original cuts so the stringers will sit flush with the face of the post. Position the posts, notches facing out. Keep notches aligned and the tops of the posts 36" above the ground. Be sure there is 7½" between the bottom notch and the ground.

3 Set the posts in concrete. Fit a 73½" stringer into the notches in the first pair of posts. Position it to cover the entire notch in the first post and half of the notch in the second. Attach the stringer with 2" galvanized deck screws. Install the other two stringers for this pair of posts. Butt a stringer against the first one and attach it securely. Repeat with remaining stringers.

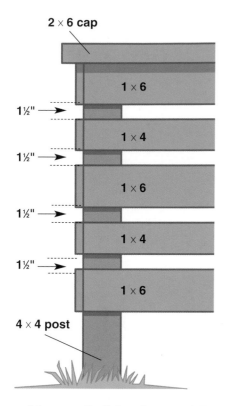

2 × 6 cap

1 × 6

1½"

1 × 4

1½"

1 × 6

1½"

1 × 4

1½"

1 × 6

4 × 4 post

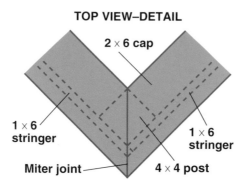

TOP VIEW–DETAIL

2 × 6 cap

1 × 6 stringer

1 × 6 stringer

Miter joint

4 × 4 post

Everything You Need:

Tools: Tape measure, reciprocating saw or handsaw, combination square, circular saw, drill.

Materials: Lumber (see Cutting List), 2" galvanized deck screws, 3" galvanized deck screws, paint, stain, or sealer.

Cutting List

Each 72" bay requires:

Part	Type	Size	Qty.
Posts	4 × 4	66"	2
Stringers	1 × 4	72"*	2
	1 × 6	72"*	3
Top cap	2 × 6	72"*	1

*add 1¾" to end post stringers and top cap

How to Build a Capped Post & Rail Fence

1 Mark the fence line, spacing posts 72" on-center. Cut the lumber to length and finish. Dig postholes and set the posts. Measure and mark each post at 36" from the ground. Trim the tops. Mark a line down the center of the outside face of each post as illustrated above (except the end or gate posts). Measure from the reference line on one post to the line on the next. For each bay, cut two 1 × 4s and three 1 × 6s to this length. For the last bay, measure from the last reference line to the outside edge of the end post.

2 Position a 1 × 6 against the faces of two posts with its top edge flush with the top of the posts and its ends flush with the reference lines. Clamp the stringer in place, then attach it on both ends with 2" galvanized deck screws. On each post, mark a line 1½" from the bottom of the 1 × 6. Use a scrap piece of lumber to make a spacer. Secure the lower strings with screws. Alternate 1 × 6s and 1 × 4s, spacing them 1½" apart.

3 Measure and cut 2 × 6s to fit between post tops. Add 1¾" on the end posts so the cap stringers extend beyond the posts. For corners, cut the ends at 45° angles, using a circular saw. Position a cap stringer on the post tops, flush with the back of the posts and extending 1¼" beyond the front. Make sure the ends are centered on the posts and attach the caps, using 3" galvanized deck screws.

159

Installing a Vinyl Fence

Made of polyvinyl chloride (PVC), the same durable material as vinyl house siding, vinyl fencing is virtually maintenance free. It will never rust, rot, peel, splinter, or crack. The material itself never needs painting and is UV resistant, so it's unlikely to fade.

Most vinyl fence products are installed in the same general way, but there are some differences among details. It's important to read and follow the manufacturer's instructions precisely. Many manufacturers also provide toll-free numbers where you can get additional advice and help if necessary.

Vinyl fence materials are precut to length and shipped in unassembled kits. The prerouted holes in the posts make it easy to insert and lock the pieces together.

It's essential to reinforce each corner, end, and gate post with concrete and rebar. If the fence is 60" or higher, it's a good idea to reinforce each of the posts. If concrete were allowed to seep

into the stringers, it would cause them to sag over time. To prevent that problem, tape or plug the ends of each stringer before installing it.

Since most vinyl fencing is ordered directly from the manufacturer or through a distributor, you'll have an opportunity to ask questions before you place an order. Lay out your fence line and consider any special challenges, such as slope issues. With that information in hand, a sales representative may be able to help you customize the materials and simplify the installation process.

Everything You Need:

Tools: Cordless drill or screwdriver, level.

Materials: PVC vinyl fencing materials, duct tape, #3 rebar, rebar separator clips, construction adhesive.

How to Install Vinyl Fencing

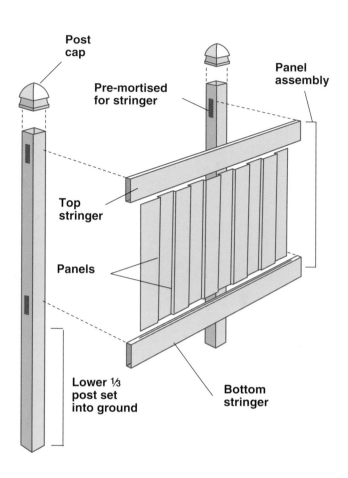

Post cap

Pre-mortised for stringer

Panel assembly

Top stringer

Panels

Lower ⅓ post set into ground

Bottom stringer

1 NOTE: These are general installation tips. Refer to the manufacturer's instructions for your specific fence style. Mark the fence line, spacing postholes according to manufacturer recommendations. Dig postholes. Place tape over the ends of the lower stringers so concrete cannot seep into them from the posts.

2 Insert the panel pieces into the prerouted holes of the bottom stringer. Make sure each piece fits securely. If not, add duct tape to the bottom of the pieces so the fit is tighter. Attach the top stringer to the panels, making sure the fit is tight. Work from one end and adjust the panel pieces to fit into the prerouted holes. Secure the stringer to the panels with the self-tapping screws provided by the manufacturer.

(continued next page)

3 Position the first post. Because the posts are manufactured to size, the posts must sit precisely at
the height of the fence. If a post is too high, lay a
board over the top and gently tap it down. If it's too
low, add gravel beneath it. Leave enough room for a
2" gap between the bottom of the fence and the
ground. Mix concrete and set the post. Use a level on
adjacent sides to check that the post is plumb. Keep
the posts plumb with 2 × 4 braces attached to stakes
driven into the ground. Duct tape is strong enough to
hold the braces to the vinyl posts without causing any
damage. Let the concrete cure at least two days.

4 Set the next post and pour the concrete footing
but do not brace the post just yet. With the assis-
tance of another person, fit the panel between the
posts. Insert the top and bottom stringers to the prerouted holes of the first (previously set) post. Insert
the stringers on the other end of the panel into the
next post. If necessary, adjust the post to accommodate the stringers.

**Shown cut
away for clarity**

5 Inside the post, drive a screw (provided with the
kit) through the top stringer to secure it. Plumb the
post and brace it with 2 × 4s. Repeat this procedure
of setting a post, then attaching a panel. Plumb each
post and brace it securely in place before you begin
work on the next panel.

6 If you're installing a gate, mount the hinge and
latch hardware to the gate posts. Attach the gate.

Shown cut away for clarity

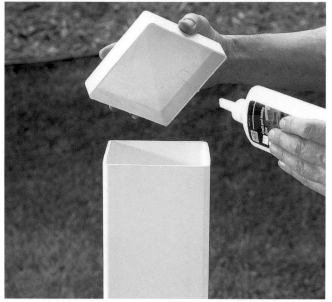

7 Connect two 72"-lengths of #3 rebar with rebar-separator clips for every end and corner post. Place one clip 6" down from the top of each piece and another 12" up from the bottom. Position the rebar assembly inside the post, with the pieces of rebar sitting in opposing corners. Fill the post with concrete, leaving at least 6" of exposed rebar at the top. Wipe off any excess concrete.

8 Attach post caps with glue or screws, if provided by the manufacturer. If you use glue, apply it to the inside edge of the cap, and then attach the cap to the post top. Wipe off any excess glue as soon as possible. Cover exposed screw heads with screw caps if provided. Wash the fence with a mild detergent and water.

Variation: Louvered fences filter sightlines, providing privacy without completely obscuring the view. They are perfect for extremely windy climates—their variated structure diffuses wind very effectively.

Installing a Chain-link Fence

If you're looking for a strong, durable, and economical way to keep pets and children in—or out—of your yard, a chain-link fence may be the perfect solution. Chain-link fences require minimal maintenance and provide excellent security. And for yards that include slopes, it's a natural choice—the mesh flexes enough that it can be adjusted to follow the contours of most yards.

A 48"-tall fence—the most common choice for residential use—is what we've demonstrated here. The posts, fittings, and chain-link mesh, which are made from galvanized metal, can be purchased at home centers and fencing retailers. The end, corner, and gate posts, called terminal posts, bear the stress of the entire fence line. They're larger in diameter than line posts and require larger concrete footings. A footing three times the post diameter is sufficient for terminal posts.

The fittings are designed to accommodate slight alignment and height differences between terminal posts and line posts. Tension bands, which

hold the mesh to the terminal posts, have one flat side to keep the mesh flush along the outside of the fence line. The stringer ends hold the top stringer in place and keep it aligned. Loop caps on the line posts position the top stringer to brace the mesh.

When the framework is in place, the mesh must be tightened against it. This is done a section at a time with a winch tool called a come-along. As you tighten the come-along, the tension is distributed evenly across the entire length of the mesh, stretching it taut against the framework. One note of caution: It's surprisingly easy to topple the posts if you over-tighten the come-along. To avoid this problem, tighten just until the links of the mesh are difficult to squeeze together by hand.

For added stability, you can weave a heavy-gauge wire through the mesh, approximately 4" above the ground. Pull the wire taut and secure it to brace bands placed on the terminal posts.

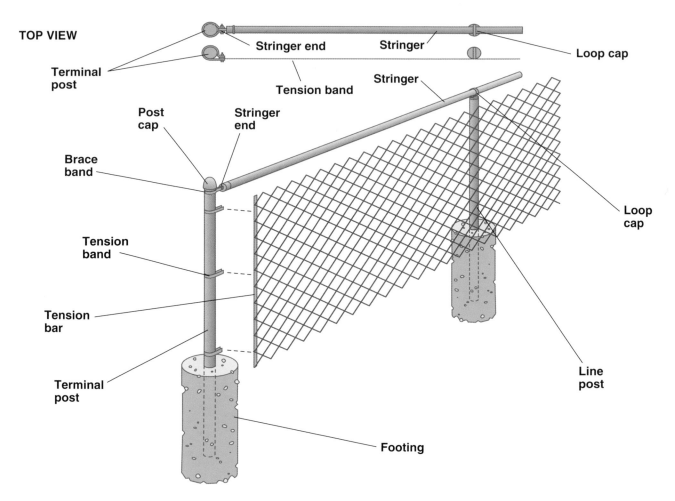

TOP VIEW

Terminal post

Stringer end

Stringer

Loop cap

Tension band

Stringer

Post cap

Stringer end

Brace band

Loop cap

Tension band

Tension bar

Line post

Terminal post

Footing

How to Build a Chain-link Fence

Everything You Need:

Tools: Tape measure, mason's string, stakes, chalk, wrench & pliers, hacksaw or pipe cutter, heavy-duty work gloves, come-along (fence stretcher), duct tape.

Materials: Galvanized terminal and line posts, galvanized fittings (see diagram), bolts & nuts for chain link fence assembly, galvanized chain link mesh.

1 Measure and mark the post locations with stakes, every 96" on-center. For terminal posts (end, corner, and gate posts), dig the postholes 8" wide; for line posts, 6" wide. Set in concrete. Each terminal post should be 50" above the ground, or 2" above the fence height. Plumb each post, and brace it on adjacent sides with stakes and scrap pieces of 2 × 4 taped securely to the post. From the top of each terminal post, measure down 4" and mark with chalk. Run a mason's string between the posts at the reference marks. Fill the line postholes with concrete. Keep the post tops level with the mason's string, or 46" above the ground. Plumb each post and brace it on adjacent sides. Let the concrete cure for two days.

(continued next page)

2 Place three tension bands on every gate and end post. Place the first band 8" from the top, the second 24" from the top, and the third 8" off the ground. Make sure the flat side of each tension band faces the outside of the fence and points into the fence bay.

3 For corner posts, use six tension bands, two bands at each location. Point the flat sides of the bands in opposite directions. Place a brace band approximately 3" below the top of each terminal post. Connect a stringer end to the brace band. The angled connection side of the stringer end should face down. Make sure the head of the bolt faces the outside of the fence line. For corners, place two brace bands on top of one another. Connect a stringer end to the upper brace band so the angled connection side points upward, and one to the lower brace band so the angled connection side points downward.

4 Top each terminal post with a post cap and each line post with a loop cap. Make sure the loop cap openings are perpendicular to the fence line, with the offset side facing the outside of the fence line.

5 Start at one section, between two terminal posts, and feed the nontapered end of a top stringer through the loop caps, toward a terminal post. Insert the nontapered end into the cup of the stringer end. Make sure the stringer is snug. If necessary, loosen the brace band bolt and adjust it. Continue to feed pieces of top stringer through the loop caps, fitting the nontapered ends over the tapered ends. Use a sleeve to join two nontapered ends if necessary.

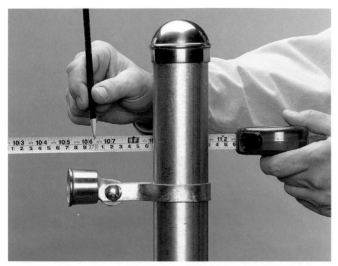

6 To fit the last piece of top stringer in the section, measure from where the taper begins on the previous piece to the inside back wall of the stringer end cup. Cut a piece of top stringer to size, using a hacksaw or pipe cutter. Connect the nontapered end to the tapered end of the previous stringer. Loosen the brace band bolt and insert the cut end to the stringer end assembly. Make sure the fittings remain snug. Repeat for each section of the fence.

7 Unroll chain-link mesh on the ground and stretch it along the fence line, from terminal post to terminal post. Weave a tension bar through the end row of the mesh. Secure the tension bar to the tension bands on the terminal post with bolts and nuts. Make sure the bolt heads face the outside of the fence. Pull the mesh taut along the fence line by hand, moving toward the terminal post at the other end. Set the mesh on end and lean it against the posts as you go.

Come-along

8 Weave the spread bar of a come-along through the mesh, about 48" from the final post, then hook the come-along to the tension bar. Attach the other end of the come-along to the terminal post, near the middle. Tighten slowly, until the mesh is taut. Keep the top of the mesh lined up, so that the peaks of the links rise 1" above the top stringer. Pull the remaining mesh tight to the post by hand, and insert a tension bar where the mesh meets the tension braces. Remove any excess mesh by bending back the top and bottom knuckle ends of one zig-zag strand in the mesh. Spin the strand counterclockwise so it winds out of the mesh. Secure the tension bar to the tension bands with bolts and nuts, with the bolt heads facing the outside of the fence. Use tie wire spaced every 12" to attach the mesh to the top stringer and line posts. Repeat for each section.

Variation: If a section of chain-link mesh comes up short between posts, add another piece by weaving two sections together. With the first section laid out along the fence line, estimate how much more mesh is needed to reach the next post. Detach the amount of mesh needed as described in Step 8. Place this new section at the short end of the mesh so the zig-zag patterns of the links line up. Weave the new section into the other section by reversing the unwinding process. Hook the end of the strand into the first link of the first section. Spin the strand clockwise until it winds into the first link of the second section, and so on. When the strand has connected the two sections, bend both ends back into a knuckle. Attach the chain link mesh to the fence framework.

Building a Custom Gate

The instructions shown here give the basics of building a solid, durable custom gate. Two methods are shown: Z-frame and perimeter frame. A Z-frame gate is ideal for a light, simple gate, while a perimeter-frame gate is necessary for larger, more ornate gates. In both styles, the diagonal brace must run from the bottom of the hinge side too the top of the latch side, to provide support and keep the gate square.

To operate correctly, a gate's weight must be properly distributed, with solid post footings that prevent sagging.

The two gates featured here show techniques that can be adapted for many gate styles. There are many hinge, latch, and handle styles available. Choose the largest hinges available that are in proportion to your gate, and a latch or handle that meets the gate's purpose and your style preferences.

Z-frame gate is simple to build.

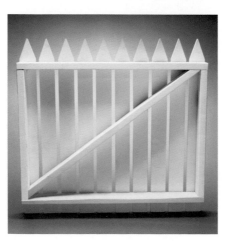

Perimeter-frame gate is sturdier.

How to Build a Z-Frame Gate

1 Check both posts for plumb and measure the gate opening. Consult your hinge and latch hardware for necessary clearances, and subtract that amount from the opening width. Cut 2 × 4s to this length. Paint, stain or seal, the lumber for the gate and let it dry.

2 Measure the distance between the top and bottom stringers on the fence. Cut two 2 × 4s to this length to use as supports. Lay out the frame with the supports between the braces. Square the corners with a framing square. Place a 2 × 4 diagonally across the frame and mark and cut it to length. Screw the brace into position with 2½" deck screws.

3 Plan the lay out of the siding to match the fence. Clamp a 2 × 4 against the bottom brace. Align the first and last boards and attach them to the frame using pairs of 2" deck screws. Attach the rest of the siding using spacers as necessary.

4 Shim the gate into position and mark the locations for the hinges. Drill pilot holes and install the hinges. Hang the gate with the hardware provided and install the latch hardware according to the manufacturer's instructions.

How to Build a Perimeter-Frame Gate

1 Follow Step 1 for a Z-frame gate (page 169). Measure the distance between the top and bottom stringers on the fence. Cut two 2 × 4s to this length for the vertical braces. Lay out the frame and secure the pieces with 2½" deck screws.

2 Position the frame on a 2 × 4 set on edge running diagonally from one corner to the other. Use scrap 2 × 4 to support the frame. Mark and cut the diagonal brace to length using a circular saw set to the desired bevel angle. Screw the brace into position with 2½" deck screws.

3 Clamp a scrap 2 × 4 to the bottom edge to use as a guide. Align the first and last siding boards flush with the edges of the vertical braces. Attach the boards with 2" deck screws. Align and attach the rest of the siding using a spacer. Mount the hardware and hang the gate as for a Z-frame gate (page 169).

Variation: Dress up your gate with inset accent pieces. This gate has a frame with a horizontal support to allow the inset of a stained glass window.

Prefabricated Gate Options

Chain-link gates are available in a small range of sizes and styles at home centers. Specialty retailers may offer more options.

Custom iron gates are best suited to large landscapes and should match the fencing materials used, as in this estate-sized property.

Painted aluminum gates are a lightweight option that can blend well with any fence style.

Vinyl fencing manufacturers offer a surprisingl wide selection of custom gates to help you individualize your fence and landscape.

How to Build an Arbor Gate

1 Measure the opening between the gate posts and determine the finished size of your gate and trellis. Compare your dimensions to the ones in the Cutting List on page 172 and make any necessary adjustments. (The tie beams for the trellis should be about 32" longer than the width of the gate.) Cut the lumber for the trellis and gate. Paint, stain, or seal the pieces on all sides and edges. Let them dry thoroughly. Lay out one side of the trellis, following the diagram on page 173. Mark the cutting lines and cut the joints, then set the frame back together. When you're satisfied with the layout and sure the frame is square, secure the joints, using two 2½" galvanized deck screws in each joint. Repeat preceding steps to build the remaining trellis frame.

2 Referring to the diagram on page 173 and to your own gate measurements, mark the positions of the trellis frame on the ground, using stakes and string. Make sure the layout is square by measuring from corner to corner and adjusting the stakes until these diagonal measurements are equal. Set one trellis frame into position, with the inside face of the frame flush with the inside face of the gate post. Drive a 24" pressure-treated stake behind the opposite side of the frame to hold the trellis in position. Drill three evenly spaced pilot holes through the frame and into the gate post. Attach the frame to the post, using 3" galvanized lag screws. Repeat steps to attach the other trellis frame to the opposite post.

3 Check the position of the free sides of the frames and measure the diagonals to ensure that the layout is square. Clamp each frame to its stake and check and adjust the frame for level. When the trellis frame is level, drill pilot holes and attach the frames to the stakes, using 2" lag screws.

4 Using the grid method or a photocopier, enlarge the pattern (page 173), and transfer it to a large piece of cardboard. Cut out the pattern, then trace the shape onto the ends of each 2 × 4 tie beam. Cut the beams to shape, using a jig saw. Mark and cut the lap joints as described in Step 1. Sand the cut surfaces, then touch them up with paint, stain, or sealer and let them dry. Position a tie beam flush with the top of the post. Clamp the beam into place and drill pilot holes through it and into each post. Drive five 1½" galvanized deck screws into each joint to attach the tie beam to the posts. Repeat preceding steps to install the remaining tie beam.

5 Hold a 2 × 2 in position between the tie beams, flush with the tops of the beams and centered between the ends of the trellis frame. Drill pilot holes through the tie beams, one into each end of the rafter; secure the rafter with 2½" galvanized deck screws. Repeat, placing four evenly spaced rafters across the span of the tie beams.

(continued next page)

6 Set a millwork bracket into place at each of the corners between the tie beams and the trellis frame posts. Drill pilot holes and secure the brackets, using finish nails.

7 Lay out the parts of the gate frame and measure from one corner to the diagonally opposite corner. Repeat at the opposite corners. Adjust the pieces until these measurements are equal and the frame is square. Secure each joint, using $1\frac{1}{2}$" galvanized deck screws. Position a 2 × 4 so that it runs from the bottom of the hinge side of the frame to the first horizontal brace on the latch side. Mark the angle of the cutting lines, then cut the brace to fit, using a circular saw. Use $2\frac{1}{2}$" galvanized deck screws to secure the brace into position.

8 Clamp a 2 × 4 across the bottom of the frame to act as a reference for the length of the pickets. Position the siding flush with the lower edge of the clamped 2 × 4. Align the right edge of a 1 × 6 flush with the right edge of the frame. Drill pilot holes and attach the siding to the frame, using $1\frac{1}{2}$" galvanized deck screws. Set scraps of $\frac{5}{8}$" plywood in place as spacers, then add a second 1 × 6. Continuing to use the $\frac{5}{8}$" plywood as spacers, cover the remainder of the frame with 1 × 4 siding.

9 Measure and mark the hinge positions on the gate. Drill pilot holes and drive screws to secure the hinges to the gate. On the handle-side post, clamp a 1 × 2 in place to act as a stop for the gate. Shim the gate into position, centered within the opening. Use a carpenter's level to make sure that the gate is level and plumb and that the stop is properly positioned. Mark the position of the stop and set the gate aside. Drill pilot holes and secure the stop to the post, using 2½" galvanized deck screws. With the gate shimmed back into position, mark the hinge-side post to indicate the hinge screw locations, then drill pilot holes. Fasten the hinges to the post, using the screws provided with the hinge hardware.

10 Cut a piece of flexible PVC pipe 52½" long (or 12" longer than the width of your gate). Clamp the PVC pipe at the top of the outside edges of the last piece of siding on each side of the gate. Tack a nail just above the first horizontal brace of the frame at the center of the gate. If this happens to be between two pieces of siding, set a scrap behind the siding to hold the nail. Adjust the PVC pipe until it fits just below the nail and creates a pleasing curve. Trace the curve of the PVC pipe onto the face of the siding. Remove the pipe and cut along the marked line, using a jig saw. Sand the tops of the siding and repair the finish as necessary. Mark the handle location on the gate. Drill pilot holes and secure the handle, using the screws provided by the manufacturer.

Brick pillars are a substantial and attractive addition to any landscape. Using these plans, it's possible to create garden pillars with different decorative or functional qualities. The columns are ideal for framing stairs or fences, but there are many possibilities. Build three or four pillars in graduated sizes to create a terraced effect. Use pillars as pedestals around the garden to highlight large pots full of cascading blooms or favorite outdoor statuary. Build short pillars that act as the base of an arbor or outdoor bench.

Building Brick Pillars

Nothing gives a landscape a greater sense of permanence and substance than well-planned and well-executed masonry work. It makes the impression that the structures will be there for decades, not just a few summers. And masonry doesn't have to mean just simple projects like walking paths or borders around your plantings. If you're feeling ambitious, you can tackle a bit of bricklaying.

As masonry projects go, this one is fairly simple. Even if you're a beginner, you can build these elegant, professional-looking pillars if you proceed slowly and follow the instructions carefully. Of course, if you have a friend or relative who knows his (or her) way around brick and mortar, it can't hurt to have an experienced eye check out your progress.

Your adventure in bricklaying begins with choosing a site for the pillars and pouring footings to support them. These below-grade columns of concrete provide a stable foundation that will protect your pillars when freezes and thaws

cause the soil to shift.

The finished pillars can serve many functions. They can support a gate, frame a flower bed of which you're particularly proud, or support meandering vines. Whatever their primary purpose, you'll enjoy them for years, perhaps decades, as they weather and gain character. And you'll be proud to tell everyone that you built them.

Everything You Need

Tools: Mason's string, shovel, wheelbarrow, pencil, masonry trowel, level, jointer, tape measure, circular saw, hand maul.

Materials: Rope, stakes, 2 × 4s, 2 × 2, 1 × 2, concrete mix, standard modular bricks (4 × 2⅔ × 8"), type N mortar mix, small dowel, vegetable oil, ½" wire mesh, 2 capstones, ⅜" plywood scraps, 2½" deck or wallboard screws, ⅜"-thick wood scraps.

Building Brick Columns

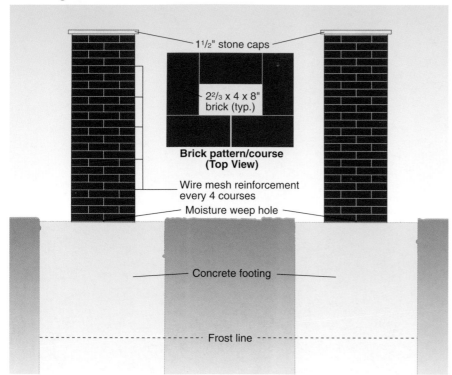

1½" stone caps

2⅔ x 4 x 8" brick (typ.)

Brick pattern/course (Top View)

Wire mesh reinforcement every 4 courses

Moisture weep hole

Concrete footing

Frost line

Brick columns are built on wide concrete footings. Wire mesh placed every four courses reinforces the columns, while weep holes at the bottoms allow moisture to drain. Stone caps can be custom ordered from a stone supplier. Have them cut so they overlap the columns by 1½".

1 Mark the pillar locations. Make an outline of each footing. Then lay out a 16 × 20" footing for each pillar with mason's string. Strip away sod. Dig a hole for each footing to code-mandated depth, using the mason's strings as guides. Following the layout, build 16 × 20" forms (interior dimensions), using 2 × 4s and screws. Sink the forms into the ground slightly so the visible portions of the footings will look neat and provide a flat, even surface for laying bricks. Drive stakes outside the 2 × 4s to support the form. Adjust the forms until they're level and square.

2 Mix the dry concrete with water, following the manufacturer's instructions. Pour the concrete into one footing hole, filling it to the top of the form. Screed away any excess concrete with a 2 × 4. The surface of the footing should be smooth and even. Repeat the process for the other footing. Let the concrete cure for at least two days before removing the forms and building on top of the footings. Waiting a week is even better.

(continued next page)

3 A story pole allows you to check the positions of the courses of brick and the thickness of the mortar joints. Build a story pole by cutting spacers from ⅜" plywood. On a worksurface, lay out 10 or more courses of brick. With the bricks on their sides, insert spacers between each pair, spacing them ⅜" apart. Place a straight 1 × 2 alongside the bricks; then mark the space between each pair of bricks, indicating location and thickness of each layer of mortar.

4 After the footings have cured, arrange five of the bricks to form a rectangle on one of the footings. Insert spacers between the bricks to establish the thickness of the vertical mortar joints. Take care that the bricks are correctly centered on each footing and square in relation to each other. With a grease pencil or carpenter's pencil, draw reference lines on the footing around the bricks.

5 Trowel mortar within the reference lines to a thickness of ⅜". Apply ⅜" of mortar to the sides of alternating bricks, so that mortar fills the spaces between them, and set the bricks on the mortar bed, tapping each gently with the trowel handle. On one side of the pillar, use a pencil coated with vegetable oil to make a weep hole in the wet mortar between two bricks. When all five bricks in the first course are laid, check for square and level, and adjust bricks by tapping them with the trowel handle.

6 Apply mortar to the top of the first course of bricks, ⅜" thick. Lay the second course of brick in the mortar, but rotate the pattern 180°. Check the pillar with a level, making sure your work is both level and plumb. Adjust bricks as necessary. Then, use the story pole as a guide to make sure the two courses on all sides are correctly spaced. Small errors made low on the pillar will be exaggerated with each successive course. Check your work after every two courses of brick.

7 Proceed with the next two courses and apply mortar to the top of the fourth course. Then cut a piece of ¼" wire mesh slightly smaller than the dimensions of a course of bricks and lay it into the mortar for lateral reinforcement. Apply more mortar to the top of the wire mesh, and lay the fifth course of brick. Add wire-mesh reinforcement after every fourth course.

8 After the fifth course, use a jointer to tool the mortar joints. Continue to lay bricks until the next-to-last course. Apply mortar to the next-to-last course, and add wire mesh. Apply mortar to the entire surface of the wire mesh. Lay the side of the last course formed by two bricks. Then add an extra brick in the center, over the mortar-covered wire mesh. Lay the remaining bricks so they fit snugly around the center brick. Tool any remaining joints as they become firm.

9 Lay the first course of brick, following the instructions in Steps 5 and 6 on page 180. Measure the distance between the pillars with a tape measure. Make a measuring rod by cutting a 2 × 2 or other straight board to match the distance between the bases of the two pillars. Use the rod every few courses to check that the second pillar is aligned with (parallel to) the first. Also, consult the story pole after every two courses. Complete the second pillar, following the instructions in Steps 4 through 8.

10 Draw diagonal reference lines from corner to corner on the bottoms of the capstones. Then, using the dimensions of the pillar and the diagonal lines, draw a rectangle centered on the bottom of each capstone. Apply a ½"-thick bed of mortar to the pillar and place the capstone. Tool the mortar flush with the brick. NOTE: If mortar squeezes out, press ⅜"-thick shims into the mortar on each side to support the cap. After 24 hours, tap out the wood scraps and fill in the spaces with fresh mortar

Building a Brick & Cedar Fence

This elegant fence is not nearly as difficult to construct as it looks. It does, however, require some time and effort, and will make use of both your carpentry and masonry skills. There are also quite a few necessary materials, which does increase the expense. But when the project is complete, you'll have an attractive, durable structure that will be the envy of the neighborhood.

The 72" brick pillars replace the posts of most fences. The footings need to be 4" longer and wider than the pillar on each side, 16 × 20" for this project.

To maintain an even ⅜" mortar joint spacing between bricks, create a story pole using a 2 × 2 marked with the spacing. After every few courses, hold the pole against the pillar to check the joints for a consistent thickness. Also make sure the pillars remain as plumb, level, and square as possible. Poor pillar construction greatly reduces strength and longevity of the pillars.

Attaching the stringers to the pillars is fairly easy. Brackets and concrete screws are available that have as much holding power as lag bolts and anchors. Although other brands are available, we used ¼"-diameter concrete screws. The screws come with a special drill bit to make sure the embedment holes are the right diameter and depth, which simplifies the process for you.

The part of this project that looks the trickiest is creating the arched top of the cedar-slat fence sections. It can be achieved relatively easily by using a piece of PVC pipe. With the ends anchored, the pipe is flexible enough to bend into position and rigid enough to hold the form of the arch so it can be traced.

Everything You Need

Tools: Brick pillar tools (page 178), tape measure, level, drill, circular saw, hammer, jig saw.

Materials: Brick pillar materials (page 178), chalk, 2 × 6 fence brackets (6 per bay), 1¼" countersink concrete screws, concrete drill bit, pressure-treated, cedar, or redwood lumber, 1 × 6, 8 ft. (16 per bay), 2 × 6, 8 ft. (3 per bay), 1½" stainless steel deck screws, 1½" finish nails (3), 96"-length of flexible ¼" PVC pipe.

Cutting List

Each 96" bay requires:

Part	Type	Size	Qty.
Stringers	2 × 6	96"	3
Siding	1 × 6	72"	16

How to Build a Brick & Cedar Fence

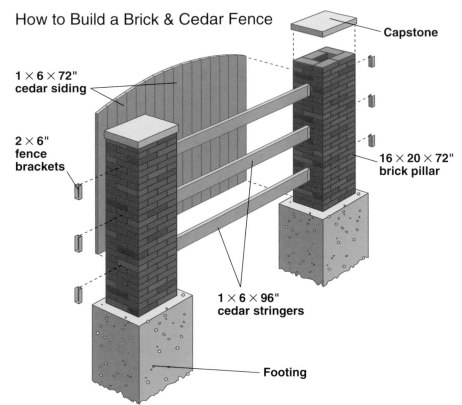

Capstone

**1 × 6 × 72"
cedar siding**

**2 × 6"
fence
brackets**

**16 × 20 × 72"
brick pillar**

**1 × 6 × 96"
cedar stringers**

Footing

1 On the inner face of each pillar (the face perpendicular to the fence line), measure down from the top and use chalk to mark at 18", 36", and 60". At each mark, measure in 6¾" from the outside face of the pillar and mark with the chalk. Position a 2 × 6 fence bracket at the point where the reference marks intersect. Mark the screw holes on the pillar face, two or three per bracket. Drill 1¾"-deep embedment holes at each mark, using the bit provided with the concrete screws. The hole must be ¼" deeper than the length of the screw.

2 Align the fence bracket screw holes with the embedment holes, and drive the 1¼" concrete screws into the pillar. Repeat for each pillar, attaching three fence brackets on each side of each line pillar. Measure the distance from a fence bracket of the first pillar to the corresponding fence bracket of the next to determine the length of the stringers. Mark and cut cedar 2 × 6s to length. Insert 2 × 6 stringers into each pair of brackets and secure with 1½" stainless steel screws.

3 Lay out 16 1 × 6s, with ½" of space between them and the cut ends flush. On the end boards, mark 64" from the bottom. Tack a nail into each mark. Snap a line between the nails. At the center, mark a point 6" above to indicate the top of the arch. Place a 96" length of flexible PVC pipe against the two nails. At the mid-point, bend the pipe up to the top mark. Drive a nail to hold the pipe in place and trace the pipe to form the arch. Cut the arch along the marked line.

4 Run a mason's string 2" above the bottom of the fence line as a guide. Attach the siding to the stringers, using 1½" stainless steel deck screws. Maintain a 2" gap at the bottom of the fence and make sure the boards are plumb. Use ½" scraps of wood as spacing guides between boards. Repeat for each section of fence.

How to Build a Brick Arch (continued)

Variation: If your existing pillars are topped with cap-stones, remove the caps before building the arch. Chip out the old mortar from underneath, using a hammer and joint chisel. With a helper nearby to support the cap, use a pry bar and shims to remove each cap from the pillar.

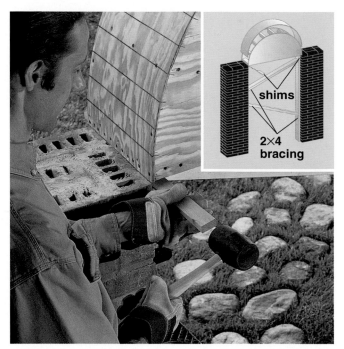

3 Place shims on top of each 2 × 8 to raise the form so its bottom is even with the tops of the pillars. Rest the plywood form on the braces. Cut two 2 × 8 braces, ½" shorter than pillar height, and prop one against each pillar with 2 × 4 cross braces.

4 Mix mortar and trowel a narrow ⅜" layer on top of one pillar. Place one brick, then rap the top with a trowel handle to settle it. Butter the bottom of each subsequent brick, and place it in position.

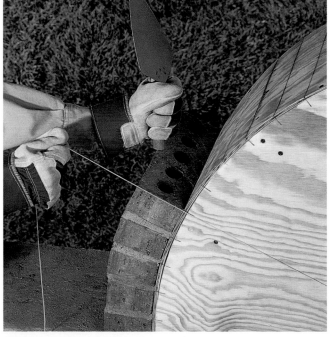

5 Once you've placed five bricks, tack a string to the center point of the form on each side and use the string to check each brick's alignment. Switch to the other side of the form and place more bricks, to balance the weight on the form. Continue to place bricks on alternate sides, until one brick remains. Smooth previous joints with a jointing tool as they become firm.

6 Butter the final brick in the first course, the center brick or *keystone*, as accurately as possible and ease it into place. Smooth the remaining joints with a jointing tool.

7 Lay a bed of mortar over the first course, then lay the second course halfway up each side. Maintain the same mortar joint thickness as in the first layer. Some of the joints will be staggered, adding strength to the arch.

8 Dry-lay several more bricks on one side—using shims as substitutes for mortar joints—to check the amount of space remaining. Remove the shims and lay the final bricks with mortar, then smooth the joints with a jointing tool.

9 Leave the form in place for a week, misting occasionally. Carefully remove the braces and form. Tuck-point and smooth the joints on the underside of the arch

Building a Concrete Block Garden Wall

In some regions, mortared concrete block walls stand sentry at the borders of many yards. They're a durable, economical way to provide privacy and security. In some situations their utilitarian look is just what's called for, but in others a little decorative flair is in order. Adding decorative blocks as shown above or covering the blocks with stone veneer as shown on page 191 adds some style to these perennial favorites.

The wall we demonstrate here is 36" tall. If you're planning a taller wall, you'll have to reinforce it by adding rebar and filling the block hollows with mortar. And, of course, a concrete block wall requires a footing that is twice as wide as the wall and reaches at least 12" below the frost line. Check your local building codes for installation requirements for both the wall and the footings before you begin this or any block project.

There are three basic block types: Stretcher blocks have flanges on both ends and are used to build the body of the wall. End blocks are smooth on one end with flanges on the other. They are used for the wall ends and corners, with the smooth face out. Half-blocks are also used to achieve the proper staggered block pattern. When using any type of block, make sure the side with the wider flanges is facing upward. These wider flanges provide more surface for the mortar.

Laying block is a matter of applying mortar to the footing and blocks and positioning them properly—proper positioning is the key to the strength and durability of a block wall. Keep in mind that although laying block isn't difficult, it is heavy work. If possible, recruit a friend or two to help you.

Everything You Need

Tools: Stakes & mason's string, tape measure, hammer, pencil, circular saw with a masonry-cutting blade, chalk line, line level, wheelbarrow or mortar box, mason's trowel, 4-ft. carpenter's level, V-shaped jointing tool.

Materials: Mortar mix, 8 × 8" concrete blocks (end, stretcher, & cap), ⅜" wood strips or dowels.

For Variation: Wire lath, self-tapping masonry anchors, stone veneer.

Buttering a concrete block involves laying narrow slices of mortar on the two flanges at the end of the block. It is not necessary to butter the valley between the flanges unless the project calls for it.

How to Build a Mortared Block Wall

1 Plot the wall line with stakes and mason's string. Outline the footings and measure the diagonals to make sure the outline is square. Adjust if necessary. Dig the trenches and pour the footings as described on page 147.

2 Test-fit a course of blocks on the footing, using end and stretcher blocks. Use ⅜" wood strips or dowels as spacers to maintain even gaps for the mortar. Cut blocks as necessary, using a circular saw and masonry-cutting blade. Mark the ends of the course on the footing, 3" from the blocks. Remove the blocks and set them nearby.

3 Mix mortar in a wheelbarrow or mortar box. (The mortar should hold its shape when squeezed with your hand.) Dampen the center of the footing, then trowel thick lines of mortar, slightly wider and longer than the base of the end block.

4 Set an end block into the mortar, with the end aligned with the pencil mark on the footing. Set a level on top of the block, then tap the block with a trowel handle until it's level. Use the chalk line as a reference point for keeping the block in line.

5 At the opposite end of the footing, apply mortar, then set and level another end block. Stake a mason's string flush with the top outside corners of the end blocks. Check the string with a line level, and then adjust the blocks to align with the string. Remove any excess mortar and fill the gaps beneath the blocks.

(continued next page)

How to Build a Mortared Block Wall (continued)

6 Apply mortar to the vertical flanges on one side of a standard block and to the footing. Set the block next to the end. Place and line it up with the string.

7 Trowel a 1" layer of mortar along the top flanges of one end block of the first course. Scrape off any mortar that falls onto the footing. Start the second course with a half-sized end block, which will offset the vertical joints. Keep the blocks plumb and aligned with the mason's string.

Vertical joints

Variation: If the wall includes a corner, begin the second course with a full-sized end block placed to span the vertical joint formed at the junction of the two runs. Build up three courses of the corners as you build the ends.

8 Install the second course of blocks, using the same method as with the first course. Scrape off excess mortar and tool the joints with a jointing tool. Install each additional course of blocks by repeating this process. Finish the joints as each course is completed. Use a level to make sure the wall remains plumb.

9 Apply mortar to the top of the finished wall. Ease the end (and corner, if necessary) cap blocks into position. Place them gently so their weight doesn't squeeze the mortar out of the joints. Make sure the cap blocks are level and plumb, using a 4-ft. level.

Variation: When building stack bond walls with vertical joints that are in alignment, use wire reinforcing strips in the mortar beds every third course (or as required by local codes) to increase the strength of the wall. The wire should be completely embedded in the mortar.

Applying Stone Veneer

If a mortared block wall fits into your plans, but you don't like the appearance, you can set stone veneer over the finished wall.

Start by attaching wire lath to the entire surface of the wall, using self-tapping masonry anchors.

Next, apply a ½"-thick layer of mortar over the lath. Scratch grooves into the damp mortar, using the trowel tip. Let the mortar dry overnight.

Apply mortar to the back of each veneer piece, then press it onto the wall with a twisting motion. Start at the bottom of the wall and maintain a ½" gap between pieces. Let the mortar dry for 24 hours.

Fill the joints with fresh mortar, using a mortar bag. Use a V-shaped jointing tool to finish the joints.

Stone veneer can dress up the surface of a block wall. Veneer, which is lightweight and easy to handle, is available in many styles and colors. Shaped end and corner pieces greatly simplify the process of setting it.

4 Fill any significant gaps between the shaping stones with filler stones.

5 Lay the stones for the second course corner so they cover the joints of the first course corner. Form corners using the same steps as for forming the first course corner. Use stones that have long, square sides. Build up the corner two courses high. Place tie stones across the width of each wall just before the corner. Build the wall ends in this same way. Use stones of varying lengths so that each joint is covered by the stone above it. Wedge filler stones into any large gaps.

6 Lay the third course. Work from the corner to the end of the wall. If necessary, shape or split the final stones of the course to size with a masonry saw or hand sledge and chisel. Place tie stones every 36". Lay shaping stones between the tie stones. Make sure to stagger the joints; stones of varying lengths will help offset them. Continue to place filler stones into any cracks on the surface or sides of the wall. Continue laying courses, maintaining a consistent height along the wall and adding tie stones to every third course. Check for level as you go.

7 When the wall is about 36" high, check for level. Trowel mortar onto the center of the wall, keeping it at least 6" from the edges. Center the capstones and set them as close together as possible. Carefully fill the cracks between the capstones with mortar. Let any excess mortar dry until crumbly, then brush it off. After two or three days, scrub off any residue using water and a rough-textured rag.

Dry Stone Wall Variation: Slopes & Curves

If the wall goes up- or downhill, step the trench, the courses, and the top of the wall to keep the stones level.

If slope is an issue along your wall site, you can easily build a stepped wall to accommodate it. The key is to keep the stones level so they won't shift or slide with the grade, and to keep the first course below ground level. This means digging a stepped trench.

Lay out the wall site with stakes and mason's string. Dig a trench 4" to 6" deep along the entire site, including the slope. Mark the slope with stakes at the bottom where it starts, and at the top where it ends.

Begin the first course along the straight-line section of the trench, leading up to the start of the slope. At the reference stake, dig into the slope so a pair of shaping stones will sit level with the rest of the wall.

To create the first step, excavate a new trench into the slope, so that the bottom is level with the top of the previous course. Dig into the slope the length of one-and-a-half stones. This will allow one pair of stones to be completely below the ground level, and one pair to span the joint where the new trench and the stones in the course below meet.

Continue creating steps, to the top of the slope. Make sure each step of the trench section remains level with the course beneath. Then fill the courses, laying stones in the same manner as for a straight-line wall. Build to a maximum height of 36", and finish by stepping the top to match the grade change, or create a level top with the wall running into the slope.

If you'd like a curved wall or wall segment, lay out each curve, as demonstrated on page 142. Then dig the trench as for a straight wall, sloping the sides into a slight V toward the center. Lay the stones as for a straight wall, but use shorter stones; long, horizontal stones do not work as well for a tight curve. Lay the stones so they are tight together, offsetting the joints along the entire stretch. Be careful to keep the stone faces vertical to sustain the curve all the way up the height of the wall.

© Crandall & Crandall this page

To build a curved wall, lay out the curve, using a string staked to a center point as a compass. Then, dig the trench and set stones using the same techniques as for a straight wall.

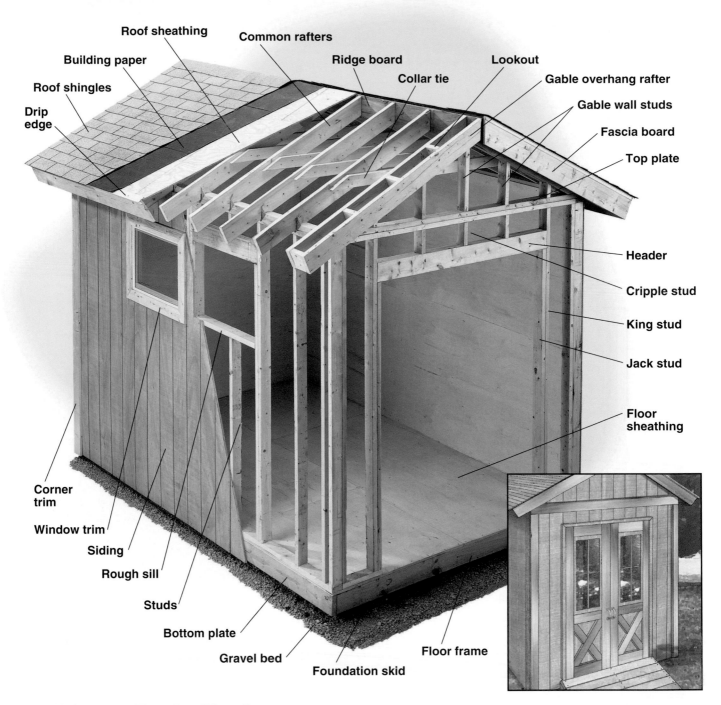

Roof sheathing

Building paper

Roof shingles

Drip edge

Common rafters

Ridge board

Collar tie

Lookout

Gable overhang rafter

Gable wall studs

Fascia board

Top plate

Header

Cripple stud

King stud

Jack stud

Floor sheathing

Corner trim

Window trim

Siding

Rough sill

Studs

Bottom plate

Gravel bed

Foundation skid

Floor frame

Building a Basic Shed

A shed can have many functions in a landscape, from providing basic storage space to creating space for pursuing a hobby. The simple design of this 8 × 12-ft. shed makes it easily adaptable for different uses.

This design features a double French door designed for a 5 ft. 2" rough opening, and two windows—one 32" square, the other, 32" x 64". The shed design can (and may need to be) adapted to the window and door dimensions of the units you purchase. It's a good idea to buy your pre-hung windows and doors first, then carefully review their dimensions and make changes to your shed plan if necessary. You many choose to install a sliding patio door, for example; or a single security door. You can also change the window sizes and locations to fit your needs.

The finishes on this shed are also very basic—asphalt shingles and rough plywood siding. You can very easily customize the finishes to your preferences. Cedar shakes, for example, could be used to finish the roof.

Materials

Description	Quantity/Size	Material
Foundation		
Drainage material	1.4 cu. yd.	Compactible gravel
Skids	3 @ 12'-0"	4 × 4 treated timbers
Floor Framing		
Rim joists	2 @ 12'-0"	2 × 6 pressure-treated
Joists	10 @ 8'-0"	2 × 6 pressure-treated
Floor sheathing	3 sheets, 4 × 8'	¾" tongue-&-groove ext.-grade plywood
Joist clip angles	20	3" × 3" × 3" × 16 gauge galvanized
Wall Framing		
Bottom plates	2 @ 12'-0" 2 @ 8'-0"	2 × 4
Top plates	4 @ 12'-0" 4 @ 8'-0"	2 × 4
Studs	40 @ 92⅝"	2 × 4
Headers	2 @ 10'-0", 2 @ 6'0"	2 × 6
Header spacers	1 @ 9'-0", 1 @ 6'-0"	½" plywood—5" wide
Gable Wall Framing		
Top plates	2 @ 8'-0"	2 × 4
Studs	2 @ 8'-0"	2 × 4
Roof Framing		
Rafters	18 @ 6'-0"	2 × 6
Metal anchors—rafters	10, with nails	Simpson H1
Rafter ties	3 @ 8'-0"	2 × 4
Ridge board	1 @ 14'-0"	2 × 8
Lookouts	1 @ 8'-0"	2 × 6
Subfascia	1 @ 8'-0", 2 @ 10'-0"	2 × 6
Soffit nailers	3 @ 8'-0"	2 × 2
Exterior Finishes		
Plywood siding	10 sheets @ 4 × 9'	⅝" texture 1-11 plywood siding, grooves 8" o.c.
Z-flashing	2 pieces @ 8 ft.	Galvanized—18- gauge
Wall & corner trim	10 @ 10'-0"	1 × 4 S4S cedar
Fascia	8 @ 8'-0"	1 × 8 S4S cedar
Plywood soffits	2 sheets @ 4 × 8'	⅜" cedar or fir plywood
Soffit vents	4 @ 4 × 12"	Louver with bug screen
Flashing (door/window trim)	8 linear ft.	Galvanized—18-gauge
Roofing		
Roof sheathing	6 sheets @ 4 × 8'	½" ext.-grade plywood
Asphalt shingles	150 sq. ft.	250# per square (min.)
15# building paper	150 sq. ft.	
Metal drip edge	2 @ 14'-0", 4 @ 6'-0"	Galvanized metal

Description	Quantity/Size	Material
Door, 5 ft. R.O.	Preframed patio door or French door	
Exterior trim	2 @ 8'-0", 1 @ 6'-0"	1 × 4 S4S cedar
Interior trim (optional)	2 @ 8'-0", 1 @ 6'-0"	1 × 2 S4S cedar
Strap hinges	6, with screws	Exterior hinges
Windows (2)	32" square	
	32" x 64"	
Exterior trim	5 @ 8'-0"	1 × 4 S4S cedar
Interior trim (optional)	5 @ 8'-0"	1 × 2 S4S cedar
Ramp (Optional)		
Pads	2 @ 6'-0"	2 × 8 pressure-treated
Stringers	1 @ 8'-0"	2 × 8 pressure-treated
Decking	7 @ 6'-0"	2 × 4 pressure-treated
Fasteners		
16d common nails	16 lb.	
10d common nails	1 lb.	
10d galvanized casing nails	1 lb.	
8d common nails	½ lb.	
8d box nails	3 lb.	
8d galvanized box nails	1½ lb.	
8d galvanized finish nails	7 lb.	
⅞" galvanized roofing nails	2 lb.	
3d galvanized box nails	¼ lb.	
1½" joist hanger nails	80 nails	
1¼" wood screws	70 screws	
3½" deck screws	12 screws	
3" deck screws	50 screws	
2½" deck screws	40 screws	
1¼" deck screws	30 screws	
Silicone-latex caulk	1 tube	

Building Section

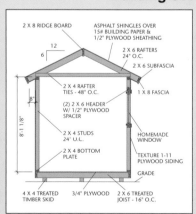

2 X 8 RIDGE BOARD

ASPHALT SHINGLES OVER 15# BUILDING PAPER & 1/2" PLYWOOD SHEATHING

12
6

2 X 6 RAFTERS 24" O.C.

2 X 6 SUBFASCIA

2 X 4 RAFTER TIES - 48" O.C.

1 X 8 FASCIA

(2) 2 X 6 HEADER W/ 1/2" PLYWOOD SPACER

2 X 4 STUDS 24" O.C.

HOMEMADE WINDOW

2 X 4 BOTTOM PLATE

TEXTURE 1-11 PLYWOOD SIDING

8'-1 1/8"

8"

GRADE

4 X 4 TREATED TIMBER SKID

3/4" PLYWOOD

2 X 6 TREATED JOIST - 16" O.C.

Tools: Shovel, rake, 4-ft. level, straight 8-ft. 2 × 4, hand tamper, circular saw, framing square, rafter square, broom, handsaw, caulk gun, stapler, chalk line, jig saw, nail set, shims.

199

Front Elevation

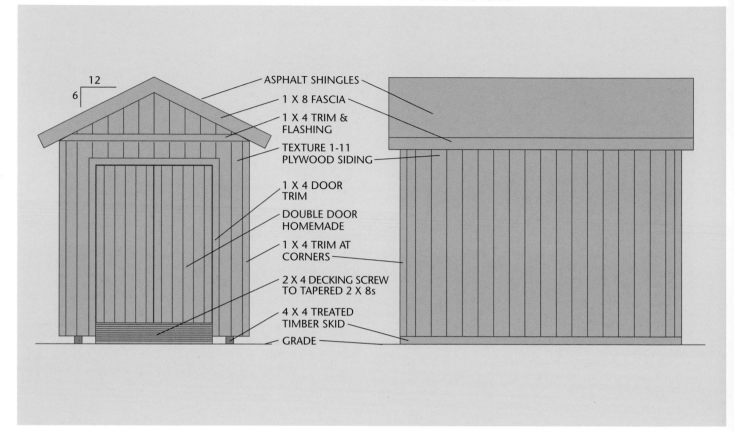

ASPHALT SHINGLES

1 X 8 FASCIA

1 X 4 TRIM & FLASHING

TEXTURE 1-11 PLYWOOD SIDING

1 X 4 DOOR TRIM

DOUBLE DOOR HOMEMADE

1 X 4 TRIM AT CORNERS

2 X 4 DECKING SCREW TO TAPERED 2 X 8s

4 X 4 TREATED TIMBER SKID

GRADE

12
6

Left Side Elevation

Rear Elevation

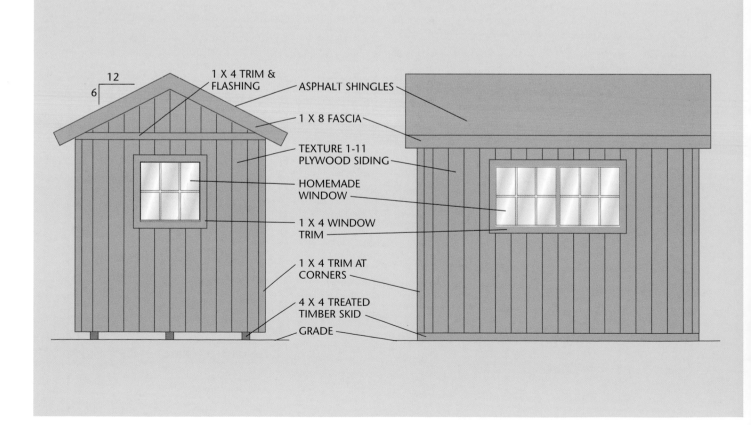

1 X 4 TRIM & FLASHING

ASPHALT SHINGLES

1 X 8 FASCIA

TEXTURE 1-11 PLYWOOD SIDING

HOMEMADE WINDOW

1 X 4 WINDOW TRIM

1 X 4 TRIM AT CORNERS

4 X 4 TREATED TIMBER SKID

GRADE

12
6

Right Side Elevation

Gable Overhang Detail

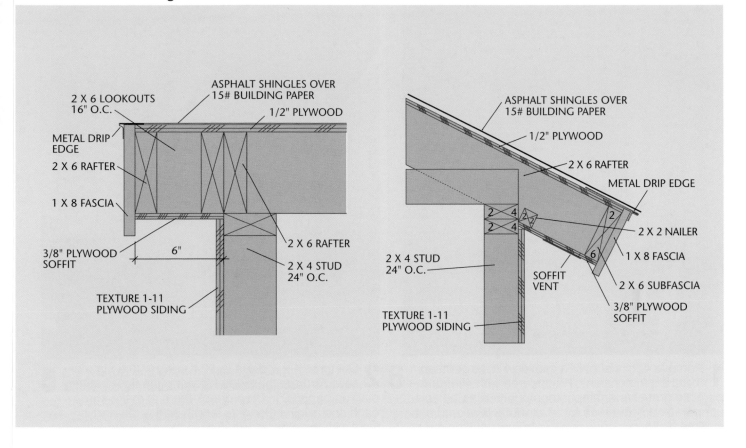

2 X 6 LOOKOUTS 16" O.C.

ASPHALT SHINGLES OVER 15# BUILDING PAPER

1/2" PLYWOOD

METAL DRIP EDGE

2 X 6 RAFTER

1 X 8 FASCIA

3/8" PLYWOOD SOFFIT

6"

2 X 6 RAFTER

2 X 4 STUD 24" O.C.

TEXTURE 1-11 PLYWOOD SIDING

Eave Detail

ASPHALT SHINGLES OVER 15# BUILDING PAPER

1/2" PLYWOOD

2 X 6 RAFTER

METAL DRIP EDGE

2 X 4 STUD 24" O.C.

2 X 4

2 X 2

2 X 6

SOFFIT VENT

TEXTURE 1-11 PLYWOOD SIDING

2 X 2 NAILER

1 X 8 FASCIA

2 X 6 SUBFASCIA

3/8" PLYWOOD SOFFIT

Window Jamb Detail

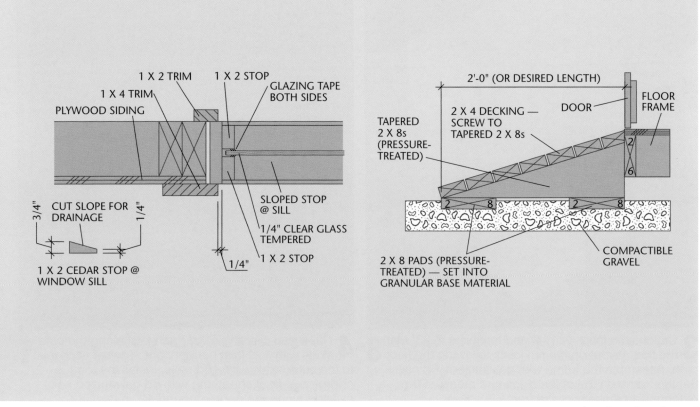

1 X 2 TRIM

1 X 4 TRIM

PLYWOOD SIDING

1 X 2 STOP

GLAZING TAPE BOTH SIDES

SLOPED STOP @ SILL

1/4" CLEAR GLASS TEMPERED

1 X 2 STOP

3/4"

CUT SLOPE FOR DRAINAGE

1/4"

1 X 2 CEDAR STOP @ WINDOW SILL

1/4"

Ramp Detail (Optional)

2'-0" (OR DESIRED LENGTH)

2 X 4 DECKING — SCREW TO TAPERED 2 X 8s

DOOR

FLOOR FRAME

TAPERED 2 X 8s (PRESSURE-TREATED)

2 X 6

2 X 8

2 X 8

2 X 8 PADS (PRESSURE-TREATED) — SET INTO GRANULAR BASE MATERIAL

COMPACTIBLE GRAVEL

(continued next page)

9 Create a duplicate of the pattern rafter. Using a scrap piece of 2 × 8, test-fit the rafters. The top cuts should meet flush with the 2 × 8 and the bird's mouth cuts should sit flush on the wall plates. Cut 12 more common rafters to size using the pattern as a guide.

10 Use the rafter template to cut four fly rafters to length without bird's mouth cuts. Cut the 2 × 8 ridge board at 156". Starting at the same end, mark the rafter layout on the wall plates and ridge board following the Framing Elevations on page 200.

11 Nail a 2 × 4 to the far wall and end of the ridge board to hold it level until a few rafters are installed. Endnail the first rafter to the ridge, then toenail the second. Install the common rafters following the layout. Reinforce the bottom joints with metal anchors.

12 Cut three 2 × 4 rafter ties at 96", clipping the top corners to follow the roof pitch. Position each tie as shown in the Framing Elevations (page 200) and facenail them to the rafters with 10d nails. Toenail the ties to the top wall plates with two 8d nails.

13 Angle-cut gable top plates to run from the ridge board to the wall plates. Fasten each plate to the rafters flush with the outer face. Transfer the stud layout to the gable top plate with a level. Bevel-cut gable studs to match the roof slope and toenail them with 8d nails.

14 Mark the layout for the lookouts on the end rafters using 16" on center spacing. Cut 16 lookouts at 3" and endnail them to the end rafters with 16d nails. Fasten the fly rafters to the ridge and lookouts with 16d nails, making sure the top edges are flush.

15 Cut and install 1 × 8 fascia along the gable ends and eaves with 10d galvanized nails. Plumb-cut the peak ends and mark and miter the corners, lock nailing them with 6d nails. Use a ¾" spacer to position the fascia so it will not interfere with the roof sheathing.

16 Install plywood sheathing, spacing it ⅛" from the fascia. Nail it in place with 8d box nails spaced every 6" on the edges and 12" in the field. Make sure each end falls on a rafter, and stagger the seams of adjoining courses, trimming the panels to fit the ridge.

(continued next page)

17 Install drip edge along the eaves with 1" roofing nails. Roll out 15# building paper over the eave drip edge and staple it securely in place every 12". Overlap preceding rows by 2" and by 6" at the ridge. Trim it flush at the ends and install the remaining drip edge.

18 Install asphalt shingles so the tabs are staggered in regular patterns, with a uniform exposed area on the shingle tabs. Start at the eave edge and work your way to the ridge. To make ridge shingles, divide the tabs and trim the corners.

19 Rip the soffit panels to fit between the wall plates and fascia. Nail the panels to the underside of the lookouts and with 3d galvanized box nails Flush the panels against the fascia, as the siding will cover the seam near the wall.

20 Install plywood siding vertically, starting at the corners. Plumb each sheet as you go. Fasten them with 8d nails driven every 6" on the perimeter and every 12" in the field. Add metal flashing between rows of siding to prevent water from entering the seam.

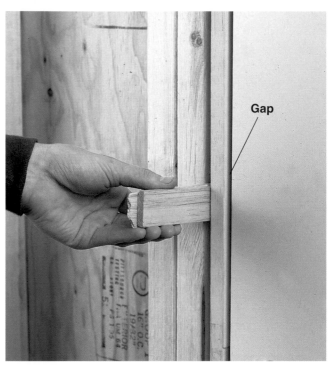

21 Cut out the bottom plate of the wall, and place the door in the rough opening. Push the brick molding against the siding and shim the door to plumb on the hinge jamb side at each hinge location. Drive 16d casing nails through the jamb and shims into the framing.

22 Shim the other jambs so the reveal is consistent and the door operates properly. Drive 16d casing nails through the jambs at shim locations. Nail through the brick molding into the framing every 16". Cut the shims flush with the framing and set all nail heads.

23 Center the window in the rough opening, shimming it so that it sits perfectly level and square. Drive one nail at each corner through the nailing flange. Check the window for smooth operation and complete the nailing according to the manufacturers instructions. Cut and install 1 × 4 window trim to cover the nailing flanges.

24 Nail two pieces of 1 × 4 together to form corner trim to cover the corner seams. Attach the trim with 10d galvanized finish nails.

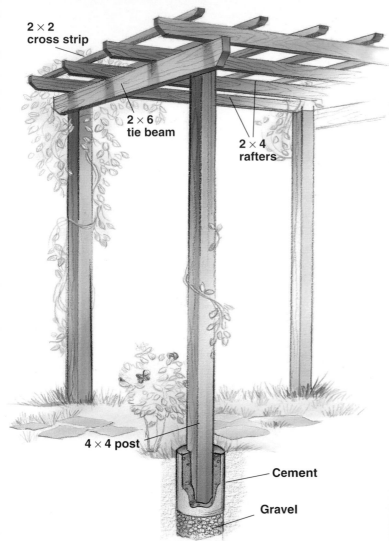

2 × 2 cross strip

2 × 6 tie beam

2 × 4 rafters

4 × 4 post

Cement

Gravel

Building an Arbor

Arbors create a lightly shaded space and add vertical interest to your landscape. For increased shade, you can cover an arbor with meshlike outdoor fabric or climbing vines. You can even transform it into a private retreat by enclosing the sides with lattice.

Our version of a post-and-slat arbor is a 5 × 5-ft., free-standing cedar structure with an extended overhead. You can easily adapt the design to different sizes, but don't space the posts more than 8 ft. apart. If you want to build a larger arbor, add additional posts between the corner posts. Before you begin construction, check your local Building Code for footing depth requirements and setback restrictions.

If you want to add climbing vines, such as clematis or wisteria, plant one vine beside the base of each post. Attach screw eyes to the outside of the posts, then string wire between the eyes. As the vines grow, train them along the wires.

Everything You Need

Tools: Basic tools, stakes & string, line level, posthole digger, reciprocating saw, paintbrush, wood screw clamps.

Materials: Concrete mix; gravel; wood sealer/protectant; cedar, redwood, or pressure-treated 4 x 4 posts (4);cedar, redwood, or pressure-treated 2 x 6 tie beams (2); galvanized nails; cedar, redwood, or pressure-treated 2 x 2 cross strips (7); 7-ft. 2 x 4 rafters (4); galvanized deck screws; 3" lag screws (8); rafter ties (8).

Cutting List

Part	Type	Length	Qty.
Posts	4 × 4	10 ft.	4
Tie beams	2 × 6	6 ft.	2
Rafters	2 × 4	7 ft.	4
Cross strips	2 × 2	7 ft.	7

How to Build an Arbor

1 Lay out the location of the posts, 5 ft. apart, using stakes and string. Make sure the layout is square by measuring from corner to corner and adjusting the layout until these diagonal measurements are equal. Dig postholes at the corners to the required depth, using a posthole digger. Fill each hole with 6" of gravel.

2 Position the posts in the holes. To brace them in a plumb position, tack support boards to the posts on adjoining faces. Adjust the posts as necessary until they're plumb. Drive a stake into the ground, flush against the base of each 2 × 4. Drive galvanized deck screws through the stakes, into the 2 × 4s. Mix one bag of dry concrete to anchor each post. Immediately check to make sure the posts are plumb, and adjust as necessary until the concrete begins to harden. Be sure to let the concrete dry at least 24 hours before continuing.

3 Measure, mark, and cut all the lumber for the arbor. Cut a 3 × 3" notch off the bottom corner of each tie beam, a 2 × 2" notch off the bottom corner of each 2 × 4 rafter, and a 1 × 1" notch off the bottom corner of each cross strip. Position a tie beam against the outside edge of a pair of posts, 7 ft. above the ground. Position the beam to extend about 1 ft. past the post on each side. Level the beam, then clamp it into place. Drill two $\frac{3}{8}$" pilot holes through the tie beam and into each post. Attach the tie beam to the posts with 3" lag screws.

4 Use a line level to mark the opposite pair of posts at the same height as the installed tie beam. Attach the remaining tie beam, repeating the process described in step 3. Cut off the posts so they're level with the tops of the tie beams.

5 Attach the rafters to the tops of the tie beams, using rafter ties and galvanized nails. Beginning 6" from the ends of the tie beams, space the rafters 2 ft. apart, with the ends extending past each tie beam by 1 ft.

6 Position a cross strip across the top of the rafters, beginning 6" from their ends. Center the strip so it extends about 6" past the outside rafters. Drill pilot holes through the cross strip and into the rafters. Attach the cross strip with galvanized screws. Add the remaining cross strips, spacing them 1 ft. apart. Finish your arbor by applying wood sealer/protectant.

Building a Barbecue

The barbecue design shown here is constructed with double walls—an inner wall, made of heat-resistant fire brick set on edge, surrounding the cooking area, and an outer wall, made of engineer brick. We chose this brick because its stout dimensions mean you'll have fewer bricks to lay. You'll need to adjust the design if you select another brick size. A 4" air space between the walls helps insulate the cooking area. The walls are capped with thin pieces of cut stone.

Refractory mortar is recommended for use with fire brick. It is heat resistant and the joints will last a long time without cracking. Ask a local brickyard to recommend a refractory mortar for outdoor use.

The foundation combines a 12"-deep footing supporting a reinforced slab. This structure, known as a floating footing, is designed to shift as a unit when temperature changes cause the ground to shift. Ask a building inspector about local building code specifications.

Everything You Need:

Tools: Tape measure, hammer, brickset chisel, mason's string, shovel, aviation snips, reciprocating saw or hack saw, masonry hoe, wood float, chalk line, level, wheelbarrow, mason's trowel, jointing tool.

Materials: Garden stakes, 2 × 4 lumber, 18-gauge galvanized metal mesh, #4 rebar, 16-gauge tie wire, bolsters, fire brick ($4\frac{1}{2} \times 2\frac{1}{2} \times 9$"), engineer brick ($4 \times 3\frac{1}{5} \times 8$"), type N mortar, refractory mortar, $\frac{3}{8}$"-dia. dowel, metal ties, 4" tee plates, engineer brick ($4 \times 2 \times 12$"), brick sealer, stainless steel expanded mesh ($23\frac{3}{4} \times 30$"), cooking grills ($23\frac{5}{8} \times 15\frac{1}{2}$"), ash pan.

A note about bricks: The brick sizes recommended above allow you to build the barbecue without splitting a lot of bricks. If the bricks recommended here are not easy to find in your area, a local brickyard can help you adjust the project dimensions to accommodate different brick sizes.

How to Pour a Floating Footing

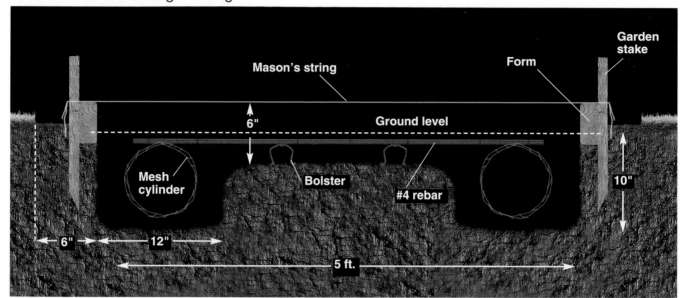

Mason's string

Form

Garden stake

6"

Ground level

Mesh cylinder

Bolster

#4 rebar

10"

6"   12"

5 ft.

Lay out a 4 × 5 ft. area. Dig a continuous trench, 12" wide × 10" deep, along the perimeter of the area, leaving a rectangular mound in the center. Remove 4" of soil from the top of the mound, and round over the edges. Set a 2 × 4 form around the site so that the top is 2" above the ground along the back and 1½" above the ground along the front. This slope will help shed water. Reinforce the footing with metal mesh and five 52"-long pieces of rebar. Use a mason's string and a line level to ensure that the forms are level from side to side. Roll the mesh into 6"-dia. cylinders and cut them to fit into the trench, leaving a 4" gap between the cylinder ends and the trench sides. Tie the rebar to the mesh so the outside pieces are 4" from the front and rear sides of the trench, centered from side to side. Space the remaining three bars evenly in between. Use bolsters where necessary to suspend the bar within the pour. Coat the forms with vegetable oil and pour the concrete.

How to Build a Barbecue

1 After the footing has cured for one week, use a chalk line to mark the layout for the inner edge of the fire brick wall. Make a line 4" in from the front edge of the footing, and a centerline perpendicular to the first line. Make a 24 × 32" rectangle that starts at the 4" line and is centered on the centerline.

Half brick

2 Dry-lay the first course of fire brick around the outside of the rectangle, allowing for ⅛"-thick mortar joints. NOTE: Proper placement of the inner walls is necessary so they can support the grills. Start with a full brick at the 4" line to start the right and left walls. Complete the course with a cut brick in the middle of the short wall.

(continued next page)

213

3 Dry-lay the outer wall, as shown here, using 4 × 3⅕ × 8" nominal engineer brick. Gap the bricks for ⅜" mortar joints. The rear wall should come within ⅜" of the last fire brick in the left inner wall. Complete the left wall with a cut brick in the middle of the wall. Mark reference lines for this outer wall.

4 Make a story pole (page 114). Mark eight courses of fire brick on the stick, leaving a ⅜" gap for the bottom joint and ⅛" gaps for the remaining joints. The top of the final course should be 36" from the bottom edge. Lay out 11 courses of engineer brick, spacing them evenly so that the final course is flush with the 36" line. Each horizontal mortar joint will be slightly less than ½" thick.

5 Lay a bed of refractory mortar (page 13) for a ⅜" joint along the reference lines for the inner wall, then lay the first course of fire brick, using ⅛" joints between the bricks.

6 Lay the first course of the outer wall, using type N mortar (page 13). Use oiled ⅜" dowels to create weep holes behind the front bricks of the left and right walls. Alternate laying the inner and outer walls, checking your work with the story pole and level after every course.

7 Start the second course of the outer wall using a half brick butted against each side of the inner wall, then complete the course. Because there is a half brick in the right outer wall, you need to use two three-quarter bricks in the second course to stagger the joints.

8 Place metal ties between the corners of the inner and outer walls, at the second, third, fifth, and seventh courses. Use ties at the front junctions and along the rear walls. Mortar the joint where the left inner wall meets the rear outer wall.

9 Smooth the mortar joints with a jointing tool when the mortar has hardened enough to resist minimal finger pressure. Check the joints in both walls after every few courses. The different mortars may need smoothing at different times.

10 Add tee plates for grill supports above the fifth, sixth, and seventh courses. Use 4"-wide plates with flanges that are no more than 3/32" thick. Position the plates along the side fire brick walls, centered 3", 12", 18", and 27" from the rear fire brick wall.

11 When both walls are complete, install the capstones. Lay a bed of type N mortar for a 3/8"-thick joint on top of the inner and outer walls. Lay the capstone flat across the walls, keeping one end flush with the inner face of the fire brick. Make sure the bricks are level, and tool the joints when they are ready. After a week, seal the capstones and the joints between them with brick sealer and install the grills.

Two methods for fire pit construction are given in this project: stucco-covered manhole block (large photo), and mortared natural stone (small photo).

Building an Outdoor Fire Pit

A fire pit creates a unique space for enjoying fun and safe recreational fires. When determining a location for a fire pit, choose a flat, level area of ground at least 25 ft. from any combustible structure. It is also important that a fire extinguisher or garden hose be nearby.

In this project there are two different fire pit finishes to choose from. The first option uses a cast concrete block known as a "manhole block." These specialty blocks are made to create rounded tunnels and walls and are available from most concrete manufacturers. The cast concrete is loose laid and then covered with a layer of surface-bonding cement, for a stucco-like texture. This cement can be tinted to match or complement your surrounding landscape features.

The second option utilizes mortared stone construction. The pit is capped with a double-wide course of smooth stones that are mortared into place and jointed.

Both options share a concrete ring footing poured directly into the ground, as well as similar construction methods for installing the

capstone. Keep in mind that building a stone fire pit requires more time to assemble and patience to construct.

After completing the project allow the pit to cure for 30 days prior to use. Heat can cause concrete with a high moisture content to crack or fragment.

Everything You Need

Tools: Hammer or hand maul, tape measure, shovel, hand tamper, wheelbarrow or mixing box, mason's trowel, spray bottle, jointing tool, square-end trowel, tuck-point trowel, circular saw with an abrasive masonry blade, eye & ear protection, wire brush.

Materials: 2 × 2 wooden stakes (2), mason's string, spray paint, compactible gravel, 60-lb. back dry concrete mix (12), sheet plastic, 6" manhole blocks or natural stone, ¾" wood spacers (3), chalk, refractory mortar, surface-bonding cement, mortar tinting agent, ½" plywood, 8 × 16" landscape pavers (10).

How to Build a Fire Pit with Manhole Block

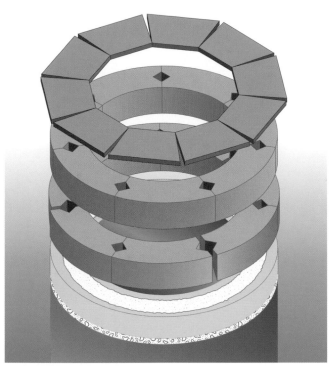

The fire pit is made up of two courses of manhole block dry-laid together and covered in surface-bonding cement. Mortar is only used to fasten the capstones in place and to set the first course of block.

1 Use a string and a stake driven into the center of the fire pit location to spray two circles 21" and 45" in diameter. Strip away the grass and dig a trench between the two circles 10" deep.

2 Pour and tamp a 2" layer of compactible gravel into the trench. Mix concrete and shovel it over the gravel, flush with the ground. Screed the concrete with a scrap 2 × 4 and float the surface with a trowel. Let the concrete dry for two to three days.

3 Remove the grass from the center of the ring and replace it with compactible gravel. Mix a batch of mortar and lightly mist the footing with water. Throw a 4"-wide bed of mortar evenly around the footing. Set the first course of block, using wood spacers at air vent locations.

(continued next page)

4 Remove any excess mortar from the first course. Dry-lay the second course of block ⅜" from the outside edge of the first course, or so the inside edges of the blocks are flush.

5 Mix a batch of surface-bonding cement and add a mortar-tinting agent if desired. Mist the surface of the walls and apply the cement with a square-end trowel. Use more cement on the second course to even out the courses. Do not cover the air vents.

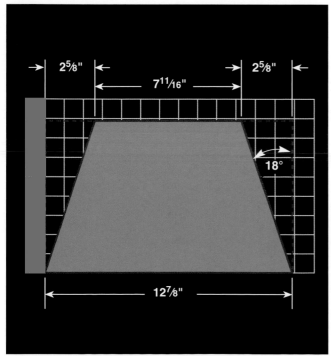

6 Make a capstone template out of plywood, following this illustration. Use the template to mark ten 8 x 16" landscaping pavers to the capstone dimensions. Cut the pavers to size with a circular saw and a masonry blade. Use a cold chisel to finish the cut.

7 Mix a batch of mortar, and fill in any block hollows, then mist the top of the fire pit with water. Lay a bed of mortar on top of the second course of block and set the capstones into place, maintaining a uniform overhang.

How to Build a Fire Pit Using Natural Stone

1 Follow Steps 1-3 on page 217. Mix a batch of mortar following the manufacturer's instructions. Mist the footing with water and set the first course of stones around the ring, maintaining a uniform distance from the outer edge of the footing.

2 Lay the first course of fire brick on the inside edge of the cut stone course. Butter the bottom and outer face of each brick with mortar and set the bricks into place, wiggling each brick slightly to set it properly.

3 Alternate, setting a course of stone followed by a course of fire brick. Stagger the seams on the stones as well as the fire brick. Continue setting courses until you reach about 18" high. Fill in any low spots between the two walls with mortar and leftover stone fragments.

4 Mix a batch of mortar and place a level, 1"-thick layer on the tops of the two walls. Set the capstones into the mortar bed, maintaining a uniform reveal around the top. Press the stones into the mortar bed. Remove the excess mortar with a rag and smooth the joints with a jointing tool.

An outdoor fireplace creates an impressive focal point for a patio or other outdoor living space. Manufactured fireplace inserts make building one easy.

Installing an Outdoor Fireplace

A custom outdoor fireplace is the ultimate focal point for a patio. Building a fireplace from real stone is a massive undertaking, and having one custom built costs many thousands of dollars. Fortunately, you can get much the same effect by building a wood framework and installing an outdoor fireplace insert. The framework is covered with stucco or veneer stone. Our installation has included both: natural stone tiles as trim pieces, with stucco covering the rest of the frame.

Fireplace inserts rated for outdoor use work much the same as their indoor cousins and can be fueled by wood or natural gas. Follow manufacturer's instructions for clearance between your fireplace and permanent structures. The unit shown here is rated to be positioned within 18" of wood siding, but always check your unit for its recommendations.

Everything You Need

Tools: Hammer, hammer drill, stapler, square-end trowel, mason's trowel, jointing tool, mortar hawk, wheelbarrow, aviation snips, utility knife, whisk broom, scratching tool (12" 2 × 2 with nails pounded through every inch).

Materials: Outdoor fireplace insert and vent piping, pressure-treated framing lumber, exterior-grade ½" plywood, 15-lb. building paper, expanded metal lath, staples, roofing nails, masonry screws, 2" galvanized deck screws, stone accent tiles, type M mortar (or mortar recommended by stone manufacturer), tuck-point mortar.

How to Build an Outdoor Fireplace

1 Build the framing for the fireplace and chimney surround. You can build it in any shape you wish; just make sure to follow setback guidelines and the firebox inset dimensions specified by the fireplace manufacturer. Begin by attaching pressure-treated 2 × 4 plates to the patio surface. Use masonry screws and construction adhesive.

2 Attach the firebox frame to the sole plates, using 3" corrosion-resistant screws. Next, build the chimney frame from 2 × dimension lumber. (Some fireplace inserts may require you to build the chimney after placing the insert in the frame.) For the chimney framing, check local code for chimney height requirements.

(continued next page)

How to Build an Outdoor Fireplace (continued)

3 Set the insert in the framing. Bend out the nailing tabs on the insert and slide the insert into the opening, maintaining even spacing on all sides. Use thin sheet-metal shims to make sure the unit is level. Secure the insert with screws as directed by the manufacturer.

4 Install the chimney vent pipe. Set the flared end of the first vent pipe section over the vent collars on top of the insert, aligning the inner and outer pipes with the vent collars. Push straight down on the pipe until it snaps into place. Assemble the rest of the vent piping.

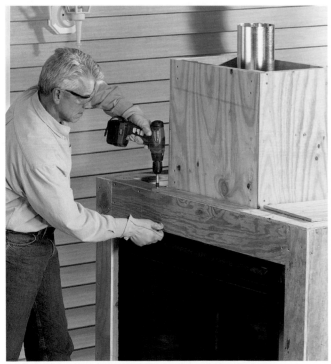

5 Once the insert and chimney are in place, install ½" exterior-grade plywood sheathing on the frame. Secure the sheathing with 2" galvanized deck screws.

6 Cover the frame with 15-lb. building paper. Overlap the edges of the paper by at least 4" and overlap corners by 16". Upper sheets should overlap lower sheets. Nail or staple the paper to the sheathing every 6".

7 Attach ¾" expanded metal lath over the building paper. Nail the lath to the frame with galvanized roofing nails every 6". Make sure the lath is nailed to the studs and that it overlaps the corners by at least 16".

8 Mix a batch of mortar and trowel a ½" to ¾" scratch coat over the entire surround and chimney framing with a square-end trowel. Take care to force the mortar into the lath. The lath should be completely covered.

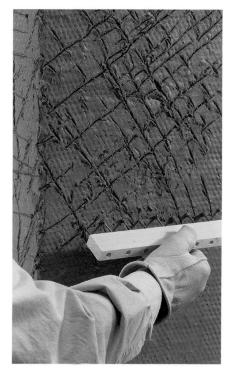

9 Before the scratch coat sets, use a homemade scratching tool or a scrap of lath to scratch grooves in the mortar. Allow the scratch coat to dry completely.

10 Mix a batch of type M mortar to apply the surface tiles to the top of the fireplace frame and the trim tiles around the edges of the firebox (see pages 130 to 137 for information on working with stone tiles). Butter the back of each tile with a ½" layer of mortar, then press in place over the scratch coat.

(continued next page)

How to Build an Outdoor Fireplace (continued)

11 Mix a finish batch of stucco that is slightly more damp than the scratch coat. If you wish, the stucco mix can be tinted to a color of your choosing. The mix should slowly drip from the trowel.

12 Mask off the trim tiles with tape. Apply the finish coat of stucco over the scratch coat, creating whatever finish you desire (see options below).

Stucco Finishing Variations

Create a float finish by covering a grout float with carpet and patting the wet surface of the finish coat.

Create a wet-dash finish by flinging (dashing) additional stucco onto the surface after the initial finish coat has dried.

Create a dash-trowel texure by flattening the wet-dash surface with a trowel.

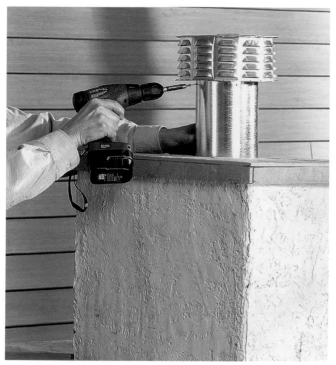

13 Install a chimney cap on the top of the chimney with sheet metal screws, following manufacturer's directions.

14 Mix grout and apply it to the joints between surface tiles on the top of the chimney box, and to the joints between the trim tiles around the firebox. You may find it easier to grout the trim tiles with a caulk gun and tube grout (inset). Remove any excess grout and smooth the joints with a moist sponge.

15 Seal the joint around the chimney and the chimney, using fireplace mortar applied with a caulk gun.

16 Install the doors or screen on the fireplace insert, following the particulars of your unit.

Flexible pond liners can be used to create an echanting watercourse of cascading waterfalls. Such a water feature is really just a series of small ponds, with a re-circulating pump that moves water back to the top pond from the bottom pond (see Variation on page 229).

Installing a Custom Garden Pond

In this first of two garden pond projects, you'll learn how to build a custom pond using flexible membrane liner that can be configured to any shape you wish. The best liners are made from rubber rather than PVC plastic, because rubber is more durable.

Garden ponds are best located on a flat building site, in a location that is not directly under a tree, but which still receives some shade. If you plan on stocking fish in your pond and you do not plan on having a filtration system, keep the numbers down to one fish per two square feet of pond surface. Replenish the water supply regularly, especially during hot, dry weather. Ponds stocked with only aquatic plants may be replenished with tap water from a garden hose. If the pond is stocked with fish, let the water sit for at least three days so any chlorine can evaporate.

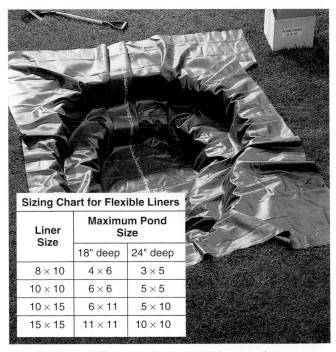

Sizing Chart for Flexible Liners		
Liner Size	Maximum Pond Size	
	18" deep	24" deep
8 × 10	4 × 6	3 × 5
10 × 10	6 × 6	5 × 5
10 × 15	6 × 11	5 × 10
15 × 15	11 × 11	10 × 10

Rainwater is a good source of water to replenish a pond, because it has no chemicals that will affect sensitive fish or aquatic plants. A rain barrel irrigation system (page 74) is one method of collection.

Flexible pond liners adapt to nearly any shape you want. Liners are available in a variety of sizes and are available in pond kits or separately. In this project a shallow shelf will hold aquatic potted plants.

How to Install a Custom Garden Pond

1 Select a site for the pond and outline the area with a hose. Avoid sharp angles, corners, and symmetrical shapes. Ponds should have at least 15 square feet of surface area. Minimum depth is 18" for plants only, 24" if fish will be added to the pond.

2 Excavate the entire pond area to a depth of about 1 ft. The sides of the pond should slope slightly toward the center. Save some of the topsoil for use with aquatic plants.

3 Excavate the center of the pond to maximum depth, plus 2" to allow for a layer of sand. Leave a 1-ft.-wide shelf inside the border to hold aquatic plants. The pond bed should be flat, with walls sloping downward from the shelf.

4 Lay a straight board across the pond, then place a carpenter's level on the board. Check all sides to make sure the edges of the pond are level. If not, adjust the surrounding ground to level by digging, filling, and packing soil.

(continued next page)

Installing a Prefabricated Pond

A very easy method of creating a landscape pond is with a rigid fiberglass liner. Rigid liners are now available in a wide range of shapes and sizes and can even be used to create a series of ponds linked by cascading waterfalls.

Rigid liners can be brittle, especially in regions with cold winters. You can minimize the chance of cracking if you work carefully to ensure that your liner is well supported with a sand base under all its surface.

The excavation for a rigid pond liner will be exactlly the same shape as your pond, tapered to fit the contours of the liner's bottom.

Everything You Need

Tools: Rope, garden spade, carpenter's level, hand spade or trowel.

Materials: Rigid pond liner, sand, flagstones.

Keep a balance of plants and fish in your pond. Floating plants provide shade for fish and help inhibit algae, but should cover no more than $2/3$ of the pond surface. Every pond should have at least one container of submerged plants, which provide oxygen for fish, for every 2 sq. ft. of pond surface. (NOTE: aquatic plants are available at local nurseries or from mail-order suppliers. Taking aquatic plants from lakes and ponds is illegal in most areas.) Fish add interest to your pond and release carbon dioxide that can be used by plants. Stock no more than one 3" fish per 2 sq. ft. of surface if your pond does not have an aeration and filtration system. After filling the pond, let water sit for at least one week before stocking it with plants and fish. Ponds with fish should be at least 24" deep.

Floating plants: no more than $2/3$ of water surface covered

Submerged plants: one container per 2 sq. ft. of water surface

Without filter one 3" fish per 2 sq. ft.

With filter two 3" fish per 2 sq. ft.

How to Install a Garden Pond with a Liner Shell

1 Set the fiberglass liner shell in place, then use ropes to outline both the flat bottom and the outside edge of the liner on the ground. Use a level to make sure the outline is directly below the outside edge of the shell.

2 Excavate the center of the site to maximum shell depth, then excavate the sides so they slope inward to the flat bottom. Test-fit the shell repeatedly, digging and filling until the shape of the hole matches the shell

3 Remove all stones and sharp objects, then set the shell into the hole. Check with a level to make sure the shell is level, and adjust the hole as necessary. The top of the shell should be slightly above ground level.

4 Begin slowly filling the shell with water. As the water level rises, pack wet sand into any gaps between the shell and the sides of the hole.

5 Dig a shallow bed around the perimeter of the liner to hold coping stones, if desired. Place the stones near the pond liner, but do not set them on the liner edges. Any weight on the edges of the fiberglass shell could cause it to crack.

Installing a Cobblestone Fountain

A cobblestone fountain is an inexpensive and easy way to add a water accent to your existing landscape. The cobblestone surface of this fountain could be cut stone or smooth river rock; the choice is yours. To eliminate weeds and help keep debris out of the basin, cover the excavated area with landscaping fabric. Set the pump up on a brick in the basin to keep it out of the residue that will collect there. Choose a submersible pump that will project water as high as you would like, but keep in mind that water that splashes out of the basin will need to be replaced.

If you want to build a fountain in an area not currently served by a GFCI-protected outlet, install one near the location or call a professional electrician.

Everything You Need

Tools: Shovel, tape measure, level, bolt cutters, metal file, hand tamper.

Materials: Plastic bucket or tub, sand, gravel, bricks (2), submersible pump with telescoping delivery pipe, landscape fabric, 9-gauge ¾" expanded metal mesh, 30 × 36", 6" paving stones (approximately 35), plants and decorative stones, as desired.

Paving stones
Expanded metal mesh
Landscape fabric
Power cord to GFCI receptacle
Basin
Submersible pump
Bricks
Excavate to thickness of paving stones plus 4"
Excavated area 30 x 36"
Sand
Soil

The simple construction and design of this fountain make it possible to place it in just about any garden corner.

How to Build a Cobblestone Fountain

1 Dig a hole the height of the basin plus the paving stones, plus 4". Cut out a 30 x 36" rectangle around the hole, two inches deeper than the stone height.

2 Add a 3" layer of gravel to the hole and then add sand tamping with the bottom of the bucket until the top of the basin is level with the paving area. Backfill the hole. Place two bricks in the bottom of the basin and center the pump on the bricks.

3 Extend the electrical cord to the nearest GFCI outlet. Lay landscaping fabric over the paving area. Fill the basin with water, turn on the pump, and adjust the flow valve to create a pleasing effect. Position the grate over the paving area.

4 Make sure the pump's water delivery tube fits through an opening in the grate. If necessary, enlarge the opening with a bolt cutter and a metal file. Set the stones in place. Leave gaps between them for water to recirculate. Arrange plants and stones to disguise the electrical cord.

Landscape Symbols

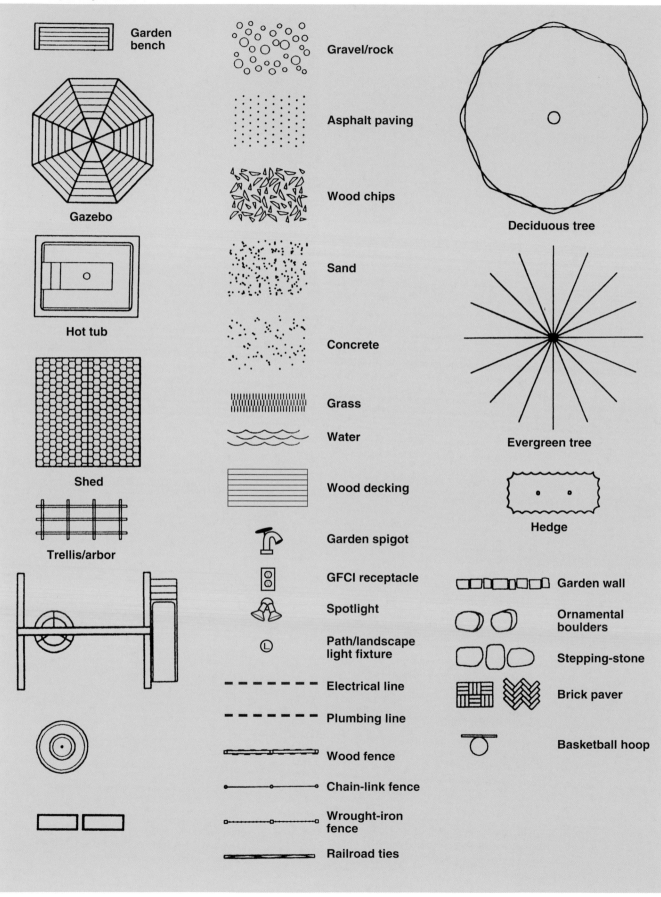

Garden bench

Gazebo

Hot tub

Shed

Trellis/arbor

Gravel/rock

Asphalt paving

Wood chips

Sand

Concrete

Grass

Water

Wood decking

Garden spigot

GFCI receptacle

Spotlight

Path/landscape light fixture

Electrical line

Plumbing line

Wood fence

Chain-link fence

Wrought-iron fence

Railroad ties

Deciduous tree

Evergreen tree

Hedge

Garden wall

Ornamental boulders

Stepping-stone

Brick paver

Basketball hoop

Product Information

Most of the products listed below are available for purchase at major home centers and many hardware stores. Refer to the listed web sites if you're looking for local distributors or need additional product information.

Composite Decking Material (p. 10)
- Trex Decking
  www.trex.com
- Timbertech Composite Decking
  www.timbertech.com

Concrete & Mortar Products (p. 13)
- Quickcrete Products Corp.
  www.quickcrete.com

Metal Connectors (p. 14)
- Simpson/Strong-Tie
  www.strongtie.com

Contractor's Calulator (p. 16)
- Calculated Industries
  www.calculated.com/productcart/pc
  /viewCat_P.asp?idCategory=16

Mason's Tools & Information (p. 19)
- National Concrete/Masonry Ass.
  www.ncma.org

Black & Decker Power Tools (p. 20)
- www.blackanddecker.com

Grading rake (p. 35)
- Rittenhouse Co.
  www.rittenhouse.ca/asp/product.
  asp?PG=1357

Drain Tile & Components (p. 38)
- Wisconsin Drain Tile Corp.
  www.draintile.com

Motion-sensor Floodlights (p. 51)
- SmartHome USA
  www.smarthomeusa.com

Outdoor Circuit Boxes & Conduit (p. 52)
- Hubbell-Bell Electrical Products
  www.hubbell-bell.com/

Low-voltage Lighting Systems (p. 64)
- Malibu Landscape Lighting
  www.usalight.com/landscape/
  default.tpl

Lawn & garden sprinkler systems (p. 68)
- Toro
  www.toro.com/watermgmt/
- Rainbird
  www.rainbird.com

Drip Irrigation Systems (p. 72)
- DripWorks
  www.dripworksusa.com
- The Drip Store
  www.dripirrigation.com
- Rainbird
  www.rainbird.com/drip/products

Rain Barrels (p. 74)
- The Great American Rainbarrel Co.
  www.greatamericanrainbarrel.com
- Gardener's Supply Company
  www.gardeners.com

Soil Testing & Gardening Info (p. 84)
- National Gardening Association
  www.garden.org/home

Wood Fence Panels (p. 150)
- Universal Forest Products
  www.ufpi.com/product/wfence

Vinyl Fence (p. 160)
- Lifetime Vinyl Fence
  www.avinylfence.com

Chain Link Fence (p. 164)
- Hoover Fence Co.
  www.hooverfence.com

Gate Hardware (p. 168)
- Hoover Fence Co.
  www.hooverfence.com

Brickwork (p. 178 to 187)
- Brick Industry Associaton
  www.bia.org

Outdoor Fireplaces (p. 220)
- HeatNGlo
  www.heatnglo-lifestyle.com

Flexible Pond Liners (p. 226)
- Pond Liners co.
  www.pondliners.com

Rigid Pond Shells (p. 230)
- Lilypons Water Gardens
  www.lilypons.com

Photo Credits

Alamy:
©Angela Jordan/Alamy: p 226 (top)

Anderson Design Services, Ltd.
Photo courtesy of Anderson Design Services, Ltd.: p. 129

Bobcat Company
www.bobcat.com
Photo courtesy of Bobcat: p. 21 (bottom left)

California Redwood Association
Redwood fence and arbor photo contributed by California Redwood Association: p. 150 (top) www.calredwood.org.

Walter Chandoha
©Walter Chandoha: p. 156

Crandall and Crandall
©Crandall and Crandall: p. 195 (both)

Creatas Images
©Creatas Images, a division of Jupiterimages Corporation: p 138

Getty Images
©Getty Images/ Photo Disc: pp. 48, 82

John Gregor
©John Gregor/ColdSnap Photography: p. 30

Saxon Holt
©Saxon Holt Photography: p. 172

Charles Mann
©Charles Mann: pp. 139 (top center), 154, 196

Jerry Pavia
©Jerry Pavia: pp. 111 (top center and bottom right), 168

Jessie Walker
©Jessie Walker: p. 106

Walpole Woodworkers
Photos courtesy of Walpole Woodworkers: p. 171 (all)

Also from

CREATIVE PUBLISHING INTERNATIONAL

IdeaWise Yards & Gardens

*D*iscover ingenious ideas and helpful how-to tips for transforming your yard into functional and beautiful outdoor living spaces.

ISBN 1-58923-159-7

IdeaWise Decks & Patios

*A*n essential information and inspiration source for creating "outdoor rooms" perfect for dining, entertaining, relaxing, and recreation.

ISBN 1-58923-178-3

Rustic Garden Projects

*R*ustic structures and accents made from green, "bark-on" woods, is the hottest trend in garden and yard décor. The projects in this book are remarkably easy to build, and most can be completed in a single weekend. Also included is information on how to find and harvest woods for construction, as well as the basic construction techniques.

ISBN 1-58923-155-4

ISBN 1-58923-159-7

ISBN 1-58923-178-3

ISBN 1-58923-155-4

CREATIVE PUBLISHING INTERNATIONAL

18705 LAKE DRIVE EAST
CHANHASSEN, MN 55317

WWW.CREATIVEPUB.COM